A
ROMANTIC
VIEW
OF
POETRY

*Being Lectures Given at
the Johns Hopkins University on the
Percy Turnbull Memorial Foundation in
November 1941*

JOSEPH WARREN BEACH

SCHOLARLY PRESS, INC.
19722 E. Nine Mile Rd., St. Clair Shores, Michigan 48080

1963

Contents

Poetry as Realization

"THE PLEASURE WHICH THERE IS IN LIFE ITSELF"

IT is not the act of living that delights us but the sense we have of the act. We do not attribute delight to the activities of the amoeba, and it was by a kind of inversion of normal statement that Arnold could say:

> 'And with joy the stars perform their shining,
> And the sea its long moon-silvered roll.

In the intensity of his realization, in the fever and fatigue of his mind, the poet could imagine no state more satisfactory than the state of unconsciousness. But the joy and self-contentment which he lent to the stars and the sea were the creation of his own thought, and unconsciousness itself could delight him only as it was conceived in his imagination. It is fit and proper· that the stars should shine and the sea should roll; in some large cosmic sense it is doubtless good that they should behave in this way. But that is a metaphysical extension of the ordinary sense of the word "good," and what is good in that sense is not the same as what gives pleasure and satisfaction to a living being like man.

I speak of satisfaction, not of distress or pain; that is the other side of the shield. We are so made that the one cannot be had without the other. And as it is no act of living that distresses us but the pain that accompanies it, just so it is, as I have said, not the act of living that delights us but the sense we have of the act.

It is life that we seek, to be sure. And life is a very comprehensive term. It includes the motion of our blood, the manifold activities of our involuntary nervous system; it includes the chemistry of the tissues and the electrical discharges throughout body and brain. We have a drive toward life as the stars have a drive toward shining and revolving. We are like a clock wound up, and the whole tension of the organism is toward further living. But when we say we seek life we are saying something more and something different. We want more life, that goes without saying. But it is not the mere gross reduplication of the process that we seek; we do not wish to live our toilsome lives twice over. It is the satisfactions that accompany every act, every state of being, the sense we have of the quality of these acts, these states, and the process of which they are a part. And poetry, as I conceive it, is the sovereign means of realizing that satisfaction which we take in living.

Poetry is not one but many things. That will be the main point of all my discourse. And I do not wish to give the impression that, in making the above statement about poetry, I fancy myself to have *defined* it. The hardest thing to do with poetry is to define it. So much of what we have to say of poetry is true of all literature, and of all fine art; and it is true of many other activities besides — like sports and games. We should not try too early to define poetry, or we shall be taking it too narrowly. We shall be ruling out many things that have always been included in it as actually practised and understood by poets, whatever critics may have to say. In this as in other investigations into fact, there is great need to go slow, as we proceed inductively, first noting the facts in all their diversity, and not to generalize except on the basis of all, or the greatest possible number of them.

But still, to begin with we need some general view, as comprehensive as we can make it, of what it is we are considering. Not a definition, but an exploratory, hypothetical formulation. We can correct and qualify as we go along,

2

and if need be we can reject it altogether if it fails to fit the facts. And so I offer, at the start, this general view of poetry as a means of realizing the satisfaction we take in living.

This does not carry us very far toward a specific definition of poetry as distinguished from other forms of speech. For I suspect that speech in general has its origin in the impulse to articulate experience in order to fix and prolong the satisfaction taken in it. Communication is something, and in all our practical affairs it is constantly employed for purely utilitarian ends. But our practical affairs are undertaken, in the long run, only to yield satisfactions that are prized on their own account. Most of our words in communication are entirely unnecessary, and a study of actual speech would probably show that nine tenths of it is motived by the simple impulse to expression. Society is a powerful incentive to the invention and use of words, and the presence of another person is an invitation to express ourselves verbally. But once words have been found, we are sure to use them even when we are alone. For we always have ourselves to talk to, and no one appreciates our own words so well as ourselves.

Poetry begins with words; and with words begin all the higher satisfactions of human experience. Mere satisfaction begins on a lower level. It begins, I am willing to say, with consciousness; with the lowest stage in animal life where the creature suffers pain or pleasure. But the monkey in the zoo running round and round in his wire hoop, while he evidently takes some pleasure in the performance, in the exercise of his faculties, has presumably little power of realizing that pleasure to himself other than by a repetition of the same act. Gesture is of course a rudimentary form of expression, and the dog's tail wagging or dragged between his legs is evidence of emotional states which in higher forms of life can be given the finer articulation of words. The cries of animals and the songs of birds are of the same kind. And where, as with dogs, there is pride and shame and personal attachment, we cannot fail to recognize a kinship with our own emotional nature. But the animals' manifestations of emotion appear to be purely automatic. It is doubtful how far even the most intelligent of them are able to take account of their own states, let alone give to them the definition, the generality, or the kind of permanency that is made possible in us by the use of verbal thought.

And so it is clear to us how much more of life we enjoy than the dog or the monkey. Ours is a vaster world, with large scope for exercises that are but dimly adumbrated in the lower animal kind. And if we are subject to sufferings and anxieties of which the dog has no inkling, that is the price we pay for a cycle of satisfactions as great in comparison with his as the solar system is great in comparison with the moon.

Shelley says of Prometheus:

> He gave man speech, and speech created thought,
> Which is the measure of the universe.

And he follows this by a recital of the arts of civilization by which, through thought, man has alleviated his slavish state — Science, which "struck the thrones of earth and heaven"; medicine, of which Disease drank and slept; astronomy, navigation, architecture — all practical and useful arts, though Shelley describes them in terms suited to the imaginative spirit of man. Still, he is thinking more of their use in alleviating man's evil state than of the satisfactions provided by them considered in and for themselves. Even music, with its office of lifting up the listening spirit, is regarded primarily as something that enables man to walk

4

"exempt from mortal care." Even poetry is viewed in its prophetic aspect, and we know what that means for the author of "Prometheus Unbound." It is poetry enlisted in the war with evil.

Well, prophecy is surely one of the functions of poetry, as freeing man from care is one of the functions of music. But these are partial views of poetry and music, and by no means do justice to the conception and practice of those arts by Shelley or Brahms or any other genuine artist. They were brought in by Shelley in a special connection, and do not cover the ground he covers elsewhere, as in his "Defense of Poetry." Speech enables us to measure the universe in other ways than those of Newton, or Kant, or John Stuart Mill. It enables us to take stock of the universe and assay its values for us as feeling beings.

And first of all, it is the means by which we *identify* the objects and experiences that make up our universe, both for their practical uses and for their esthetic qualities. By their names we distinguish oak and pine, and that not merely for their serviceability in building, or for burning in a fireplace, or (botanically) for their methods of reproduction, but likewise for their peculiar effects in the landscape — the gnarled sturdiness of the oak branches and the ranked straightness of pines like pillars, the soft bunchiness of the pine needles as the sun soaks down through them and loses itself in myriad pencilings of shadow; the different dealings of the wind with oaks and pines, rustling the oak leaves crisply and soughing through the pines; the differing charm of glades for walking where the foot treads on gray fallen leaves or on the ruddy carpet of pine needles. All this wealth of meaning is lodged in "oak" and "pine" for anyone who has learned the words and applied them to the experience. All this, and far more, once the process of association has begun to work, and these names have been linked with others — with mountains, with North and South, with park and wilderness.

So the word "pine" is the means by which a thousand esthetic experiences are brought together and fixed — for reference, for contemplation, for prolongation, for leisured relishing. But we have begun perhaps too far along the scale of human experience. We have begun with things, and we should perhaps have begun with acts. For if, according to Aristotle, the most important part of a tragedy is the fable, that is because in human experience generally it is action that is primary. Consider then what words do for us in helping us to realize the quality of our actions. Take some of the most primary and most active of verbs — run, leap, seize, strike, cling. Consider them not so much in relation to their uses and their practical effects as to the feeling tone of each. Running and leaping are subjects of pleasurable thought not merely because they are undertaken in the pursuit of game, which makes good eating. They give pleasure because they recall the animal exhilaration of the act, and more than that, the force and rightness of the body thus engaged, the co-ordination of all the members, the adjustment of means to ends. Running and leaping are a triumph in themselves, and where the mind rests upon them it rests on successful performance. This is the primary expression of the ego; and, apart from purely sensual gratification, it probably includes more of the satisfactions possible to man than any other. I am not sure but what, taken largely enough, it may include them all except the pleasures of sense. Seizing and clinging and striking bring us to grips with objects and persons opposed to our will, and the element of resistance heightens our sense of the force and skill and courage displayed.

Now, these types of action are common to all mammals, and we may assume that pleasure is taken by animals generally in the acts of running, leaping, seizing, striking, and

6

clinging. But how fleeting and evanescent must be the pleasure that passes with the act itself and leaves nothing but the carcass to be devoured and the dreamless sleep of satiety! How much better off we are, with all the words that give identity to the several acts and enable us to recall them to the mind, dwell on them in memory, and boast of them to our companions!

Such are the acts in which we engage as animals caught up in the struggle for existence. But even the lower animals have their families and federated bands. And with us, gregariousness brings with it a whole new set of actions, with words to identify them — to nurse and protect, to give and accept, to help and rescue and give thanks. For the sake of simplicity I leave out of account the words of opposite reference — to deny and refuse, to scold and harm, though these belong in the same stage of development and may be accompanied by satisfactions of their own, of great importance in the life of the imagination.

Let us confine ourselves for the moment to the more positive of the social acts. These bring us to morality, the code of social life. With the lower animals we do not call this morality, for we regard it as automatic and unconscious with them; by which we mean chiefly that they have no words to identify the elements of their behavior, to fix them in the mind and give them a being independent of the several acts involved or the mere physiological habit. They may be systemized as habit, but not as ideology. And, what is most important for our theme, they cannot presumably give delight to the mind of the individual concerned.

I need not dwell on the power of words like these to give satisfaction to the person who commands them, nor on the special degree and quality of satisfaction given by the contemplation of the acts so designated. To nurse and protect, to give and accept, to help and rescue and give thanks. In

7

all these cases the maximation of the ego is secured by action which is not purely self-regarding, but in which there is a participation of more than one person, joined by close heart-warming bonds of interest and kinship. The pleasure of the individual is reinforced by that of the recipient or confederate; the delight is reflected on another face, the sense of the value of the act is confirmed by the agreement of others. The approval of one's kind comes in to heighten one's self-congratulation. Such acts may bring a satisfaction less intense, because less simple, than leaping or striking, but it may be for all that more massive, more diffused, and more continuing.

Thus we have nouns for objects and verbs for actions which tend to fix and enlarge the satisfaction taken in our experience. And it is obvious enough how the same service may be rendered by adjectives and adverbs, which specifically name the qualities of objects and actions. How much we have gained in our esthetic life when we have found the words smooth and rough, hot and cold, sour and sweet, swift and slow; how much better account we can give, not merely to others but to ourselves, of experiences had and to be had, and clinging in our memory like a perfume! There are adjectives of many kinds, but I shall consider for the moment only those of the most primary signification, the most simply sensational in their reference. Here we are on the level of physical comfort and discomfort. And while the noblest of our satisfactions are not found on this level, these are at any rate among the most universal, the most persistent, the most deeply grounded in the experience of childhood, and the most indispensable for imaginative effect in poetry — not as the central theme of a poem, but as the complement of sensational reality which gives keenness and convincing earthiness to the effect.

The extraordinary power of "The Rime of the Ancient

Mariner" results from a combination of several elements very seldom brought together. The one I wish to stress is this of sensory appeal on the level of primary physical experience. And, along with Coleridge, I shall refer to his fellow romantics as they make their notations of things seen, heard, felt, tasted, and smelt.

There were plenty of poets before Coleridge and in his day who surpassed him in the range and nicety of their recording of what the senses bring us from external nature. In the composition of a landscape and the sensitive toning of it to a mood, especially the mood of elegiac meditation, Thomson does not fall far below Coleridge, and Collins at least once, in the "Ode to Evening," furnishes a classical touchstone, something perhaps never to be matched in its kind. In this type of modal composition Wordsworth probably offers the most frequent examples of high distinction — the opening stanzas of "Resolution and Independence," (more personal and dramatic than Collins), the opening strophe of "Tintern Abbey" (more personal and more intellectualized), and numerous passages in "The Prelude" — the following for one instance, from his account of Alpine scenery:

> The immeasurable height
> Of woods decaying, never to be decayed,
> The stationary blasts of waterfalls,
> And in the narrow rent at every turn
> Winds thwarting winds, bewildered and forlorn,
> The torrent shooting from the clear blue sky,
> The rocks that muttered close upon our ears,
> Black drizzling crags that spake by the wayside
> As if a voice were in them, the sick sight
> And giddy prospect of the raving stream,
> The unfettered clouds and region of the heavens,
> Tumult and peace, the darkness and the light —
> Were all like workings of one mind, the features
> Of the same face, blossoms upon one tree;

Characters of the great Apocalypse,
The types and symbols of Eternity,
Of first, and last, and midst, and without end.

But this is something else again — this Bachlike counterpoint of tumult and peace, of sublimity and ruin; this ethe-
real flight of the abstracting mind. And it would but show
how far we have outrun our theme if I should quote from
Shelley's "Mont Blanc" his culminating statement of much
the same thought concerning much the same landscape.

Our present concern is with things actually seen, heard,
felt, tasted, and smelt — with the physiological responses
that constitute the basic substance of all imaginative appeal.

There is a larger provision of this sort of thing in Wordsworth and Shelley and Keats than there is in Coleridge, if
you count the instances and list the categories of sensory
appeal, and if you have in mind realistic minuteness of observation. More than ten years before "Tintern Abbey"
Wordsworth had set down in "An Evening Walk" the con-
scientious observations of one well-read in Milton and the
eighteenth-century poets, and, what is perhaps still more
important, one obviously affected by the landscape painting
of his day. He describes a precipitous cliff with the minuteness of a painter and a naturalist, and then, with equal con-
scientiousness, studies the modifications of effect as the sun
goes down and the lights change.

How pleasant, as the sun declines, to view
The spacious landscape change in form and hue!
Here, vanish, as in mist, before a flood
Of bright obscurity, hill, lawn, and wood;
There, objects, by the searching beams betrayed,
Come forth, and here retire in purple shade;
Even the white stems of birch, the cottage white,
Soften their glare before the mellow light;
The skiffs, at anchor where with umbrage wide
Yon chestnuts half the latticed boat-house hide,

Shed from their sides, that face the sun's slant beam,
Strong flakes of radiance on the tremulous stream:
Raised by yon travelling flock, a dusty cloud
Mounts from the road, and spreads its moving shroud;
The shepherd, all involved in wreaths of fire,
Now shows a shadowy speck, and now is lost entire.

Ah yes, there speaks the man who was destined to be a friend of the painters Hazlitt and Beaumont — not too good a friend to William Hazlitt, of whom he did not approve — but the very good friend of Sir George Beaumont, whose picture of Peel Castle in a storm inspired the "Elegiac Stanzas" in which Wordsworth referred to "the light that never was on sea or land."

Yes, here in "An Evening Walk" a taste trained to the appreciation of degrees and aspects of light notes with pleasure the "flood of bright obscurity" which engulfs hill, lawn, and wood, the "slant watery lights" which move along the base of a precipice, and the "strong flakes of radiance" shed on the tremulous stream from the sides of skiffs at anchor. And the present-day connoisseur of either poetry or painting is delighted to find Wordsworth characterizing shadows as purple nearly a century before the impressionist painters discovered that they might actually have that color.

But this poem is not among the best or even the second best of Wordsworth's. And for one reason, because it is pure description. However it may be with painting, pure description has never been the substance of first-rate poetry. There is very little of it anywhere in Wordsworth. Shelley rather tends to description, in small streaks, as he tends to excess of figurative imagery; and in both cases it is a weakness in him to yield to something which is his forte. The trouble with pure description in poetry is that the subject described is something in which the poet participates only as an observer — something that does not affect him directly enough to make it strongly moving. It is of concern to him only as a person of cultivated taste. If we call such art a purely esthetic exercise, it is not to disparage esthetics, but simply for convenience of reference.

We are more directly concerned, we participate more as individuals, when the imagery involves bright and vivid color, which stimulates the animal spirits, or when it involves largeness of any kind; for greatness expands the heart by sympathy. And these two kinds of appeal are more frequently found combined in Shelley than in most poets. Here we have them in a landscape appropriate to dawn and hope, Asia's description of the scene at the arrival of her sister Panthea.

> The point of one white star is quivering still
> Deep in the orange light of widening morn
> Beyond the purple mountains: thro' a chasm
> Of wind-divided mist the darker lake
> Reflects it: now it wanes: it gleams again
> As the waves fade, and as the burning threads
> Of woven cloud unravel in pale air:
> 'Tis lost! and thro' yon peaks of cloudlike snow
> The roseate sunlight quivers: hear I not
> The Æolian music of her sea-green plumes
> Winnowing the crimson dawn?

In this characteristic passage from "Prometheus Unbound" the appeal is almost altogether through the visual sense, which sometimes seems less corporeal than touch or taste or smell, or even perhaps the sense of hearing. The thing becomes more personal to us as our own body is more involved, as in effects of temperature and all imagery associated with soft yielding to desire. In voluptuousness Shelley and Keats vie with one another, and it is hard to choose, though fairly easy to distinguish, between them. The sensuous effects of Keats seem more earthy, since in his case the color is more often attached to solid substances, while in

Shelley it is so much more likely to be the tenuous attribute of mist and cloud, of water and air, of elements in motion and spiritual essences. Color with Keats is likely to be indicated by terms that imply richness and massiveness of substance — gold and silver, marble and bronze — or rich luxuriousness of fabric. He is fond of banquets and banqueting halls and palaces of solid architectural magnificence. Hyperion's palace was

> Bastion'd with pyramids of glowing gold,
> And touch'd with shade of bronzed obelisks.

And when the wrathful god came home,

> On he flared,
> From stately nave to nave, from vault to vault,
> Through bowers of fragrant and enwreathed light,
> And diamond-paved lustrous long arcades,
> Until he reach'd the great main cupola.

That is gorgeous enough, vivid and substantial enough, for anyone. But it is Keats deliberately noble, consciously Miltonic, projecting himself into realms far beyond his own normal inhabiting. This is a Keats whom critics praise, and deplore the fate that cut him short before he could complete the cycle of his development. It is not the Keats most loved by the lovers of Keats; they do not find here the individual charm that enthralls them. This is not the Keats of the sonnets, the odes, and the tales of love and magic. And it is by no means the best example of what I am considering — the seduction of the reader through his senses. Let us, accordingly, examine a few passages that do recall the side of Keats in which he is so strong. Here he is in the realm of Flora and old Pan consorting with white-handed nymphs.

> And one will teach a tame dove how it best
> May fan the cool air gently o'er my rest;
> Another, bending o'er her nimble tread,

> Will set a green robe floating round her head,
> And still will dance with ever varied ease,
> Smiling upon the flowers and the trees:
> Another will entice me on, and on
> Through almond blossoms and rich cinnamon;
> Till in the bosom of a leafy world
> We rest in silence, like two gems upcurl'd
> In the recesses of a pearly shell.

Here is Keats, in the person of Isabella, indulging the luxury of sensuous grief, tending the severed head of a dead lover.

> In anxious secrecy they took it home,
>   And then the prize was all for Isabel:
> She calm'd its wild hair with a golden comb,
>   And all around each eye's sepulchral cell
> Pointed each fringed lash; the smeared loam
>   With tears, as chilly as a dripping well,
> She drench'd away: — and still she comb'd, and kept
> Sighing all day — and still she kiss'd, and wept.

Here is the soul of Keats melted down with sadness, moonlight, and birdsong, and with the fragrance of hidden flowers in the dark, till he is ready to yield luxuriously to self-pity and the nostalgia of death.

> Darkling I listen; and, for many a time,
>   I have been half in love with easeful Death,
> Call'd him soft names in many a musèd rhyme,
>   To take into the air my quiet breath;
> Now more than ever seems it rich to die,
>   To cease upon the midnight with no pain,
>   While thou art pouring forth thy soul abroad
>   In such an ecstasy!
>   Still wouldst thou sing, and I have ears in vain —
>   To thy high requiem become a sod.

Now, here is matter that concerns us all most directly, to which we all respond if we are human — that is, if we are susceptible to things soft, sweet, graceful, flowery, and inviting; if we are inclined to yield to erotic promptings, to the luxuries of languor, melancholy, and self-pity. And this gift of sensuous appeal it is, I think, that more than anything else makes Keats such a general favorite with lovers of poetry. Grant his strictly literary skill, his unique power of shaping and phrasing; grant the passion with which he associates the sensuous with more ideal elements. These gifts serve to confirm and sanctify the other; readers of a certain austerity they serve to reconcile to what is doubtless called the paganism of Keats — serve even, I suspect, to pull the wool over their eyes and make their poet "nicer" than he is.

It is sometimes alarming to think how many persons there are, most chaste of speech and habit, and most refined in sentiment, for whom this John Keats is the dearest of friends. Spirits that cannot abide the heady and religious grossness of Donne fall readily for the honied lewdness of Keats. Psychology comes along with comforting reflections to suggest how some principle of compensation, or vicarious living, operates to make his very bawdiness the support to their purity. In the poems of Keats there is a constant process of sublimation, of which we are all the beneficiaries. But what is sublimated is the simple seductions of the flesh. And wherever he takes us in the end, it is this, I think, that gives him first claim to our favor.

And yet, be it noted, in all my illustrations from Keats I have quoted but one poem that can be compared to "The Rime of the Ancient Mariner" for sureness of appeal, let alone poetic fineness in the absolute sense. There are several obvious reasons for the artistic superiority of "The Ancient Mariner" to such performances as "Sleep and Poetry," "The Pot of Basil," or "Hyperion." One of these is the more interesting story; another is the spiritual symbolism conveyed. But apart from these general themes there is the amplest provision of particular circumstances involving the most primary sensations suited to rouse in us, by sympathy, intense excitement.

You recall the situation. The mariner having slain the sacred bird, the ship is becalmed. This is the first of many terrible events. It is fearful in itself, and it is accompanied by circumstances and effects still more fearful. One of these is the sight of rottenness and of loathsome creatures round about them.

> The very deep did rot; O Christ!
>   That ever this should be!
> Yea, slimy things did crawl with legs
>   Upon the slimy sea.

If you recall your childhood, you will remember that nothing could fill you with a greater loathing than the touch or sight of organisms or substances suggestive of decay and putrefaction. Whether through actual experience of their evil and noisome effects, or through a mere instinctive revulsion, the race recoils from slimy things as promptly as from things too cold or too hot, and with a peculiar quality of repudiation. But Coleridge has given a special turn of the screw to his effect with the little phrase "did crawl with legs" — evoking many a startled encounter with snakes or centipedes. Our reactions in such cases have become the habit of our nerves, and the mere suggestion of things of this sort is bound to provoke a strong imaginative response.

But the calm at sea had results more fearful than the sight of loathsome creatures. In the long delay the drinking water had given out, and with the extreme heat this produced a plague of thirst so great that men could not even use the organ of speech.

> Water, water everywhere,
> And all the boards did shrink;

> Water, water everywhere
> Nor any drop to drink.
> . . . .
>
> And every tongue, through utter drought,
> Was wither'd at the root;
> We could not speak, no more than if
> We had been choked with soot.

Coleridge introduces at this point the phantom ship, barred like a dungeon grate where the sun peered through its ribs. This is effective in its way, but somewhat ambiguous in character, half allegory, half supernatural machinery. As machinery it is hardly needed, for the drought was sufficient to explain the death of the seamen — a fearful event in itself, which left the ancient mariner to bear alone the terrors of the sea. And now again it is the calm and the drought which, so far as physical experience goes, make up the world of the ancient mariner, and the spiritual suffering caused him by the dead men's curse is itself expressed in terms of drought.

> I look'd to heaven, and tried to pray;
> But or ever a prayer had gusht,
> A wicked whisper came, and made
> My heart as dry as dust.
>
> I closed my lids, and kept them close,
> And the balls like pulses beat;
> For the sky and the sea, and the sea and the sky
> Lay like a load on my weary eye,
> And the dead were at my feet.

The torrid heat is made more impressive by association with things cool and sweet.

> The moving Moon went up the sky,
> And nowhere did abide:
> Softly she was going up,
> And a star or two beside —

> Her beams bemock'd the sultry main,
> Like April hoar-frost spread;
> But where the ship's huge shadow lay,
> The charmed water burnt alway
> A still and awful red.

The dead men's curse upon him and the frightful experience of having the ship manned by the bodies of the dead are striking enough, and I do not doubt that supernatural terrors can be as piercing and real as those with a valid basis in the evidence of the senses. But it is, I think, the vivid complement of physical sensation that gives to this tale of the supernatural its unusual impressiveness, translating it into the language of common experience. The terror is one and indivisible. But it is the physical strain and agony that lend peculiar substance and convincingness to the supernatural terror and enable us to agree, without a moment's cavil, that the man is under a spell. He has inadvertently broken a tabu of fearful seriousness and has been the cause of the death of four times fifty living men. He is so deeply fallen from grace that he cannot even pray. He does not know the magic words to break the spell. He cannot pray, he cannot sleep, and he lives in an agony of heat and drought and sleepless remorse. It is by chance or by grace that he falls upon the counter charm. The beauty of the water snakes playing beyond the shadow of the ship, the beauty of living things in a world of death, moves him so that unawares he blesses them. At once the spell is snapped. For —

> The selfsame moment I could pray;
> And from my neck so free
> The Albatross fell off, and sank
> Like lead into the sea.

There follows what is perhaps the most impressive passage in the whole great poem. The mariner's troubles are not all over; he has much yet to suffer from the reproachful

eyes of the dead men. But for the moment, with the loosing
of the charm, all is relief and release.

> O sleep! it is a gentle thing,
> Beloved from pole to pole!
> To Mary Queen the praise be given!
> She sent the gentle sleep from Heaven,
> That slid into my soul.

> The silly buckets on the deck,
> That had so long remain'd,
> I dreamt that they were fill'd with dew;
> And when I awoke, it rain'd.

> My lips were wet, my throat was cold,
> My garments all were dank;
> Sure I had drunken in my dreams,
> And still my body drank.

> I moved, and could not feel my limbs:
> I was so light — almost
> I thought that I had died in sleep,
> And was a blessèd ghost.

> And soon I heard a roaring wind:
> It did not come anear;
> But with its sound it shook the sails,
> That were so thin and sere.

> The upper air burst into life!
> And a hundred fire-flags sheen,
> To and fro they were hurried about!
> And to and fro, and in and out,
> The wan stars danced between.

> And the coming wind did roar more loud,
> And the sails did sigh like sedge;
> And the rain pour'd down from one black cloud;
> The Moon was at its edge.

In this poem Coleridge has dealt more, and more na-
kedly, than other poets of his time, or than he has elsewhere
done himself, with certain physical sensations and states of

acute bodily distress and fear such as form the commonest experience of men in their struggle with the elements. I have hardly begun to list the types of primary physical sensation exploited by Coleridge in this poem — such as the sensation of swift motion in oneself or the elements, or of sudden change from movement to stillness and stillness to movement, from animation to deadness and from deadness to animation. I have singled out two or three types of physical distress. As the distress is acute, so is the satisfaction that we take in its removal or alleviation. Perhaps no mere luxurious pleasure can match in poignancy the deliciousness of release from pain. And here, I think, is found the secret of the rare vividness with which this poem seizes on the imagination.

The physical adventure of the ancient mariner is but the outward embodiment of a spiritual adventure which is, I suspect, the underlying theme of the poem — though it may have been buried so deep in the poet's emotional being that he was not himself distinctly aware of it. On this interpretation, the superstitious terrors of the mariner are symbolic of spiritual fears and distresses to which any religious soul is subject. You remember how the poem begins with the sudden halting of the wedding guest by the mariner, who is under a compulsion from time to time to tell his moral tale, and how in the end it returns to the wedding, the bride, and the vesper bell. One of the finest effects of the poem is the contrast between the peacefulness and security of the home village, with its normal human activities, associated with the church, and the terror, mystery, and evil of the sea. Coleridge was, of course, thoroughly familiar with folklore, and realized how commonly the sea was associated with evil — how the very crossing of water brings one under the thrall of unholy other-world powers. And he must have known how the surest antidote to the malicious sorcery of these evil powers is the church bell or anything connected with the service of the church.

Now, the church is not merely the church in the ritual-istic and supernatural sense; it is the community of the faithful, it is civil society and the home, represented here by the wedding feast. Separation from the church means exclu-sion from organized human society. In Coleridge's day, as for centuries before him, a voyage at sea was the classical case of separation from this ordered community; and it is no wonder that seamen were peculiarly subject to supersti-tious terrors, they were so far removed from normal human intercourse and from religion as an agency for exorcizing the evil powers.

But in a strict religious sense, what is it that shuts one out from the church and from human society? Is it not sin? And is not the popular tabu against the shooting of the sa-cred bird the imaginative equivalent in this poem of the re-ligious interdict against sin?

We know that Coleridge was throughout his life pro-foundly religious in the sense of recognizing that to be free from sin is a Christian's obligation to the deity. And there is much to suggest that he was from an early age troubled by the thought of himself as tainted with sin. It may well be that he was often haunted with the sense of being cut off by his own moral weakness from the consolations of religion and of normal human society, and that this has something to do with the fervor with which he pictures the spiritual solitude of the ancient mariner. The great thing in the poem is not, I feel, the somewhat ineffectual moral tag about lov-ing all things both great and small. The great thing is the sentiment of peace that comes to the wandering soul with his restoration to the bosom of the church and the commu-nity of the faithful. The mariner's compulsion to tell his tale is more than a didactic impulse; it is an impulse to confession.

And the feeling that follows is the feeling of absolution or atonement, the feeling of one who is no longer at the mercy of evil but has the good powers of the universe on his side. Of course, what makes the poem so effective is the terrors of a soul that has not yet been restored, that is still at the mercy of evil powers. This is the great imaginative reliance of the poet. But he knows how to use both terror and peace to reinforce one another by contrast, and bring his terrific presto back to a calm adagio or andante.

I have said so much about the latent theme of the poem in order that it may not be left out of account. But my main intention was to illustrate the physical realism with which he has given life to what might otherwise have been pale and spiritless. Coleridge has been summoned to exemplify the use of concrete words as means of realizing the satisfaction we take in living. I have not yet come to abstractions; and I have yet to try to give greater plausibility to my general proposition.

The Humanist and the Poets

W E have spoken of words concrete and particular as a means of identifying and dwelling on experience and making much of it. While these are doubtless the all-essential or basic words for the purpose, they are not the most precious of our instruments for interpreting life in its most distinctively human aspects. Most precious are the general and abstract words; for it is by means of these that we identify, not the particular fact of experience, the quality of the moment, but whole groups of experiences linked together by their common qualities, experiences in series referring to one another, forming a continuum in the memory — and thus, in short, we identify the memory itself and the person made one by his memory, the very psyche that is the subject of all experience and gives it its relevance and reality. It is thus that we know ourselves and our associates, friends, and foes; it is thus that we view our life as a subject for appreciation and are able to characterize it as a whole and in its several aspects.

We have first the words describing character — cunning and dullness, cowardice and courage, honesty, generosity, ingenuity, compassionateness, and cruelty. By these we trace the veins of gold or dross that run through all a man's action and together make up the map or silhouette of his personality. Hector is brave, Odysseus is cunning, Nestor is wise and eloquent. And then we have words like success and failure to gauge the effectiveness of our dealings with circumstance; and along with these, words to characterize the states of mind or attitudes with which we habitually confront the world — hope and despondency, doubt and faith, anxiety, desire, shame, exultation, determination, irritation, zest, torpor and animation, which together make up our temperament and philosophy of life. Then further, we have words to describe our attitudes to one another — love and hate, distrust and confidence — and our conception of the relations that should prevail among men — justice and freedom, equality and brotherhood. These abstractions comprise our moral philosophy, and we are never happy until we have made some effort to realize them in the concrete.

But we have words and concepts more abstract than any of these, referring not merely to us and our fellows, not merely to us in our personal experience, but also to the world in general in its essential nature. Such are beauty and ugliness, good and evil, which apply over the whole range of lesser abstractions, and rise themselves to a kind of apex in the all-inclusive word "value."

Value is all-inclusive in the subjective realm; for it is the standard by which we prize or disprize anything of which we have knowledge. But what is the source of value itself? Ah, there is the root problem of ethics and esthetics, and one hesitates to set up for an authority in matters so abstruse. However, one has one's own notions; and mine are such as seem to me the most fruitful in the interpretation of poetry. As I conceive it, all values have their origin and measure in the satisfactions they procure to human beings. The word "satisfaction" I take, of course, in a sense large enough to meet the popular objections to utilitarianism or hedonism. But once these objections are met, I do not mind bearing the odium of these systems. I have no knowledge of standards or sources of value outside ourselves; and within ourselves I cannot conceive of a standard or source of value more comprehensive than satisfaction, taken in the broadest sense.

And so we have the concept of human satisfaction, and

the abstract word to designate this concept, so paramount in the interpretation of poetry. For poetry is, I say, our chief means of realizing, of appreciating, the life we live. Much of our living is automatic and mechanical, below the level of consciousness, or hovering near that level where satisfactions hardly come into question. Much of it is secondary to other ends, undertaken only for the sake of things that follow upon it; and here the satisfactions are such accidental ones as the well-being attendant on the exercise of our faculties, or at best the pleasure taken in the sense of effective endeavor for whatever ends.

We are constantly engaged in activities that are not rewarding in themselves but are meant to secure some good beyond. Indeed, our lives are so largely made up of such secondary activities that it wearies and saddens us to reflect upon it. We wonder if we have not somewhere taken the wrong turning to have involved ourselves so deeply in mere machinery. Much of people's business is repetitious and habitual, the mere carrying forward of an impulse that has ceased to have meaning. Much of it is stupidly conceived by persons with low or lazy imaginations, or with timid philosophies that put a damper on the impulse to enjoyment, or uninstructed in the niceties of sensation or sentiment. Drudgery and routine have dulled their sense; pain and frustration have caused them to lower their demands on life and to ask only the material comforts; gross stimulants have dulled the edge of their palates, and vulgar notions of pleasure have pre-empted the ground and driven out all the finer flowers of the heart.

I do not speak of sickness and pain and death, of tragic losses and failures, of disgrace and dishonor and humiliation, which are the daily lot of human beings. Here I do not speak of them, though in the end it will be necessary to take them into account, and consider what satisfactions they may be made to yield in the strange economy of human nature and the poetic imagination. What I have in mind at present as abatements to the appreciation of life are the effects of torpor and routine, so feelingly referred to by Wordsworth when he commiserates with the child on the necessity of growing up:

> Why with such earnest pains dost thou provoke
> The years to bring the inevitable yoke,
> Thus blindly with thy blessedness at strife?
> Full soon thy Soul shall have her earthly freight,
> And custom lie upon thee with a weight,
> Heavy as frost, and deep almost as life!

We are certainly all grievously at war with our own delight. And yet I suppose there is hardly a life, among the saddest and dullest and most torpid, which has not its daily satisfactions in the little or in the large, or both, that keep it floating, as it were, on the surface of things, keep it from plunging below and losing itself forever. There is not the drabbest housewife who takes no pleasure in her chairs and tables, her pewter candlesticks and chests of drawers, symbols of order and domestic use, or in the fuchsias and geraniums ranged in the window of her little house on a back street. There are few craftsmen who take no satisfaction in the neat and skillful joining of woodwork, the discovery and fixing of trouble in the motor, the invention of some new device for promoting comfort or convenience. The world of sport and the world of business are each a succession of minor triumphs (along with the failures), occasions for the exercise and display of prowess and cunning; and he that has no other talent can exhibit patience lying in wait for fish and take pride in the suckers and sunfish he brings in for supper. Every week-end before the War millions of Americans had the solid satisfaction of winning a game with danger and brute matter, with time and space, and the forces of nature, as they drove their cars for hundreds of miles across entire commonwealths at faster speeds than trains or birds. And the godlike youth of the country have the option of turning birds and crowding into a short life more excitements and victories than Methuselah commanded in a millennium.

Every human being has at least a brief season of flowering of desire and sentiment. For some it is as violent, as gorgeous, as various as a jungle. Many find in marriage that instinct has joined them to someone — mortal, to be sure, and subject to the weakness and ludicrousness of the mortal state — and yet strangely congenial to their temperament, her weakness matching his strength, her strength his weakness. Intimacy may bring boredom and irritation, but it also brings understanding, sympathy, dependence, and an unbreakable habit of trust and confidence. Unexpected depths are discovered, delicacies as fragrant as arbutus, ideals as clear and hard as diamond. Tenderness grows from the root of passion. At first it is as slender and green as an annual, winding its graceful links round the trunk of an elm. Before one knows it, it has grown a tough and woody stem thick as a tree; it has reached the very top of the supporting elm, and is bound so tight by so many convolutions that you might as soon cut down the tree as get rid of the vine. Most men bring forth children to be a delight as infants, to mirror and duplicate and magnify themselves; to cause them grief and anxiety with every failure and error, but vastly more of pride and joy with every success and rightness. Every child is a promise of improvement on the parents' life, or at the very least continuance.

The evil man takes pleasure in his evil and in getting the best of the good. The honest man takes pleasure in his honest dealings as well as in his reputation for honesty. Iago delights in his treachery; the loyal man in his loyalty. The sober man rejoices in the meeting of obligations. There is scarce a man or woman living on whom does not rest some responsibility, and who does not meet it with a fair degree of faithfulness. No city could stand if this were not so; and every ship would founder, every pioneer would perish in the wilderness, were not the average man endowed with a certain pride in the meeting of his trust.

The youth lays out the plan of his life, and his dreams are of success in the execution of his plans. The old man looks back on the road he has followed, and sees how it winds across plain and mountain, through deserts and along the edge of chasms — through places mean and foul, but likewise among pleasant groves, and along heights of wide prospect. The happiest, according to Wordsworth, is he

> who, when brought
> Among the tasks of real life, hath wrought
> Upon the plan that pleased his boyish thought
> . . . .
>
> Who, with a toward or untoward lot,
> Prosperous or adverse, to his wish or not —
> Plays, in the many games of life, that one
> Where what he most doth value must be won.

At the end of the day one comes to his bed to the comfort of easeful surrender. But it is hard to let the tense machine run down, and for a certain time the day's doings will go on simmering gently or boiling furiously in his head. I think no man could sleep who found no satisfaction anywhere within the range of his consciousness — who was tortured by an absolute deprivation of hope or complacency and well-being of mind and body. All humankind must have, to cheat them at the end of the day, some morsel of comfort for the mind. It may be the thought of something well said or done, when all that disgusts has faded out of memory. For the mean man it will be a grudge that is harbored and hugged to the bosom like a treasure; for the most unprivileged of mortals, some sense of his own integrity, or identity of being — some last final clinging to what one is, some instinctive and irrational persuasion that for what one is there is a special sanction, or at least some excuse and pardon in the nature of things — that for him God or nature has a regard out of all proportion to what he is worth in the eyes of men and his own eyes.

Well, such, I take it, is the crude stuff of poetry. And the function of poetry is to give form and tongue to what is otherwise without meaning and value, and virtually without existence itself. The proper life of man begins when he begins to take note of his living and so to formulate it in the mind that it may be prolonged and magnified. This he may do for some practical end, so as better to control the world about him and direct his action upon it. And this is something else than poetry. Perhaps you might call it the beginnings of science. Poetry is concerned with the living itself, for its own sake, for the satisfactions which it yields directly. Its impulse is by words to catch this fleeting, elusive thing. As the instrument of consciousness it might almost be said to create the life — the real life which is in the awareness. It is at any rate a statement or restatement, a formulation, a recapitulation, of whatever is satisfying in the experience.

In this view, one can understand why Wordsworth should have said of poetry that it is "the breath and finer spirit of all knowledge." We also understand why Shelley should say that "poetry is the record of the best and happiest moments of the best and happiest minds." But Shelley does not hit the mark so nearly as Wordsworth. And while we may share his awe of genius and nobility, and acknowledge the rightness of his statement in its context, in his particular "defense of poetry," we find perhaps a note of smugness and piety in Shelley's view. His vision is a little too elevated for our purpose. He has not sufficiently in mind the humbler and more universal offices of poetry. We feel that Carlyle is nearer the mark when he says that "a vein of Poetry exists in the hearts of all men." We do not have in mind the *best* poetry, like Shelley or Matthew Arnold. We are thinking of poetry in its wild state, as something "in widest commonalty spread." I am about ready to say that, wherever there is life, there poetry is present potentially and in its rudiments. Indeed, I have said in effect that the poetry is the living, humanly speaking.

Now, I know how many questions of definition remain to be answered. How poetry stands in relation to the other arts. How it is to be distinguished from other kinds of speech, and especially from scientific, philosophical, and utilitarian modes of statement. What part the concept of beauty plays in a true account of poetry. What degrees of excellence exist within the realm of true poetry, and how they are determined and recognized. Above all, I realize that in finding the subject matter of poetry in human satisfactions, I have dodged the question of tragedy, pain, disgust, and futility, which are actually so large a part of its subject matter as practised by many of its greatest masters, leaving for later solution the riddle of how to make satisfactions out of distress and suffering.

Even so, I feel that we have done much in laying so broad a foundation for our study, and that we have approached it from the right direction — or rather, shall we say, from the point of view that is most likely to prove fruitful and illuminating. I hesitate to put upon this approach the name that properly designates it. I know with how little sympathy the word "psychology" is regarded among professional students of literature. As depositaries of a sacred tradition we have developed a conservatism not generally

characteristic of those who created the tradition, and especially of the poets upon whom we live. We are reluctant to
admit new methods, and above all new terms. There are at
least seven schools of psychology battling for recognition
and dominance in the field. And we forget, in our scorn
for a science so riddled with doubt and disagreement, that
we ourselves are in a sad state of confusion and that the
average teacher of literature, while he may have prejudices
and shibboleths in abundance and may be the devout fol-
lower of some verbal tradition, has not the effective faith to
give life to his subject and make it seem important, as music
and sociology and aeronautics are important to their dev-
otees.

It is for this reason, I suppose, that a generation ago so
great a following developed in our colleges for the critical
faith of which Paul Elmer More was the inventor and Irving
Babbitt the prophet, and that still this "new humanism"
has some standing in academic circles. It carries with it the
seriousness of an ethical system, and every pronouncement
is important, as the red label "poison" is important on a
bottle. It is a comprehensive system, applying infallibly to
anything that has been written, and nothing so well serves
to give direction and continuity to a set of lectures.

I remember Professor Babbitt well, and he was a very
good teacher. In French 6 he caused me to do more reading
than I had ever done in any foreign language, and this was
of the most practical advantage. For when I went to Paris
the following summer I, who had never spoken a word of
French in my life, was enabled to discuss terms with my
landlady in the language of La Fontaine and exchange sentiments with girls in the theater lobby in the language of
Racine.

Nor was this the only good I derived from the teaching
of Babbitt. Later I sat in on his course on the Romantic

Movement, and there I learned to put labels on bottles of poison. Professor Babbitt had the most fascinating set of labels and classified in the most systematic and philosophical manner: Individualism, Primitivism, Naturalism, *mélange des genres*. And my students have profited ever since by the notes I took. No one in a literature classroom went so deeply into the philosophy of the case; no surgeon's fingers ever probed more searchingly for pus and tumor; no doctor's ear was keener for flutterings in the ventricles of the heart. If my other teachers had been as much inclined to philosophy, I might have got beneath the skin of the Middle Ages. If Grandgent had given us the inwardness of Aquinas or Abelard. If Kittredge had not lost himself so long in a labyrinth of sources, parallels, and bibliography. If Chaucer had been subordinated a little less rigorously to the grammatical origins of the final *e*!

And yet, there was no one of my teachers that I did not like better than Babbitt, and find more human. There was none that did not seem to take more relish in the literature itself which was the subject of their lifelong study. Grandgent would roll the lines of Dante on his tongue with a marrowy sweetness that took you straight into the heart of the thing as sound. A Tuscan open *o* was for him something as delectable as the cedars of Lebanon. Neilson would chuckle over some slyness of Chaucer with a winsome merriment which I then took for lewdness, but which I have since learned to recognize as the humor which is the saving spice of wisdom and morality. And even then I knew it was the tone of a man of the world. As for Kittredge, he invested with so much gusto everything he touched that you could follow for an entire semester his study of the sources of "Gawain and the Green Knight" with never a sense of fatigue. It was one prodigious detective story. One by one under his charm the words of Shakespeare came to life.

They were brought forth from the shadowy penumbra of vagueness and error upon the calcium-lighted stage of actual Elizabethan usage. Each word was exhibited in its context in half a dozen passages from Shakespeare and his peers and played its part out on each of these miniature stages.

Unhousel'd, disappointed, unanel'd.

In one line of Hamlet we had an animated procession of philosophy, religion, and biography.

I had my taste of English 2 in the early days, before Kittredge had developed his temperamental role to its later extremes. And I and my friends enjoyed the exemption of favored pupils, not to be lightly made the butt of wit and ridicule. We smoked his strong cigars in the genial relaxation of Hilliard Street while Karl Young traced the influence of the "Filocolo" and the "Filostrato" upon the imagination of Chaucer, or Henry MacCracken illuminated the work of Lydgate. If the master corrected our pronunciation of English or Latin phrase, it was for the love of truth, and with kindly intent to save us humiliation later. It was something we shall never forget, and not even on our deathbed can we be guilty of calling any spirit a *deus ex machina*.

Some of those French romances were terribly long and blind, and I remember going to Kittredge once for help in locating a critical passage buried somewhere in the wastes of the "Pèlerinage de Charlemagne." I thought he might be glad to save me a week's work. But that was not his notion of the way to carry on independent research; he evidently thought I might pick up something useful on the way while plowing through this narrative again. At any rate he told me it was better to find my own way. It did not even occur to me that he might not himself know his way through that romance. Indeed, it did not occur to me till this very moment. I took for granted that Kittredge knew everything; that he had everything filed away in his head, or neatly ticketed in his card index.

During those Harvard years I often wanted to do more reading in later periods than could be managed within the program of a medievalist, and sometimes I would complain to my master of the limitations of his curriculum. But he told me that I would have all my life to catch up on my reading; that I might as well make my foundations firm to begin with. He gave me good advice of a practical nature. The pursuit of scholarship was a game, and one must learn to play it according to the rules if one wanted to reap success. And with regard to my ranging curiosity, my disposition already manifest to go after strange gods, he warned me that a rolling stone gathers no moss.

Of Kittredge's later performance as the prima donna of Harvard Hall I have knowledge only from fable and rumor. I judge that he dramatized a trifle vividly his role as master of a Latin school. In my day his histrionism was relatively mild, and we took it all as a part of his genial humanity. To me he was very much of a man; and he was more than a man, he was Olympian. I don't suppose Walt Disney ever heard of Kittredge, but he has given in "Fantasia" the most charming picture of him as Olympian Jove in that impudent piece which he set to the Pastoral Symphony. There he lies above Mount Olympus on his fleecy cloud, rosy as a child and bearded like a Corinthian capital. From the hands of Vulcan he languidly receives thunderbolts as they are forged and rouses himself to a playful excitement as he launches them upon a world of centaurs and cupids. They are beautiful thunderbolts, but I do not remember that much harm results. And then at last, when he is tired of this sport of the gods, he yawns and turns on his side like a child, draws the pink fleece round him, and goes back to sleep.

Very different is my picture of Babbitt, tense and hurried, his voice a bit harsh, with a heap of books before him on the desk, nervously fingering the leaves, seeking the place marked with a slip of paper. There on the marked page is the weak spot, the spreading sore. For what he is conducting is a clinic, or rather a post-mortem. The characteristic features of the Romantic Movement were all conceived as symptoms of disease. That, I believe, is what he called them himself. At any rate, that was the tone he took in regard to them. The literary effort of more than a century in Europe and America appeared to him as one vast infirmary. And the disease was more wide-spreading than that. It seemed to take in virtually the whole of imaginative literature, with the possible exception of Sophocles, who was passed because of something Greek and something stern about him which made up for his hectic and unsteady pulse. One felt that perhaps the "Art Poétique" of Boileau might win a clean bill of health, and possibly Wordsworth's "Laodamia."

One did not feel that Babbitt had any particular fondness for poetry or was at home in the world of the imagination or sentiment, as Woodberry, for example, was at home in it. I don't want to make too much of a casual slip. Hazlitt and Keats misquoted poetry almost as often as they quoted it. But they were writing generally without the book at hand, from memory, in hasty-scrawled letter or meeting a newspaper deadline. And they were not preparing an elaborate brief in a criminal prosecution, as Babbitt was in *Rousseau and Romanticism*. When Babbitt refers to William Morris in what were meant for his own words as

> The idle singer of an idle day,

he has spoiled a very fine line.

> The idle singer of an empty day

is the line as Morris wrote it, and even for the purpose of Babbitt's brief it is a hundred per cent better than Babbitt's version. Morris was, he confessed, an idle singer because the day was empty. Not merely as sound, as imagery, Morris's line is better as thought. And the case is worth citing, not as *proof* of Babbitt's insensitiveness to the niceties of thought and feeling, but as an illuminating instance of it.

The truth is that his system was not properly an esthetic but a moral system. He was, I take it, an earnest, high-minded, narrowly parochial spirit, who had presumably lost his hold on supernatural faith and desperately needed something else to take the place of the steadying power of religion. He was a man of limited energies who needed a moral sanction for the constraints he found it convenient to put upon himself. He had, one feels, a great fear of life and the life impulse in most of its forms, a shrinking from the perilous hazards of living; but he had a pride as great as his fear, and this pride required that he erect his own fears into a general system of ethics. It hardly requires the Marxian analysis, as it is called, to show why he should have found uncongenial philosophies of life based on the common interests of men as social beings, why he should have turned so fiercely on all humanitarian sentiments, all hopes of improving man's condition socially, and the secular ideal of social justice. The Marxian analysis might be applied. But psychologists of almost any one of the seven schools would find it simpler to trace his views back to some sense of guilt, some sense of weakness, which he must project out of himself onto Adam and Eve and the whole race of mortals.

The central concept of his system he found, it is supposed, in the writings of Paul Elmer More. Those who have read More's "Definitions of Dualism" in the seventh series of *Shelburne Essays* will know in what a hasty, undigested mass of bold assertions is based the tremendous doctrine of the inner check. It seems that man's being is sharply divided into two parts, often called in this school the animal and the human. The first part comprises impulses to action. These have their cause in the physical world; to these man is subject as he is a part of nature. The second part consists in the power of inhibiting these impulses; in so checking himself man is acting as a moral being and demonstrating the freedom of his will. Now, I have stated this position with greater clearness and simplicity than are found in More's prophetic discourse, and have thereby given it more plausibility than it has in the original. I may have given it something of a Kantian turn which it does not have in More and Babbitt. But you will find there is nothing in them that corresponds to the positive and germinal character of Kant's categorical imperative, which is concerned not with checking impulses but with directing and ordering them by a rational and broadly social criterion.

But let me go on with the system as it is in More. He strongly implies, and Babbitt after him, that there is something inherently questionable or even bad about the impulse to action, and something inherently noble and good in the act of checking it. For the one is associated with the eternal flux of things, with change and movement, which are somehow evil and disgusting; the other with immovability, which is somehow good and blessed. Why the one should be evil and the other good, the one to be shunned and the other sought, there is small suggestion in either More or Babbitt.

The philosophical reader will know that this is a feeble caricature of Plato; that in Plato there are sound metaphysical reasons for celebrating oneness as the sublime apex of his pyramidal system of abstractions, each series abstracting more from the particularity of that below it, until at length all particularity and differentiation give way in the supreme essence, which subsumes them all. The philosophical reader will know that there is something of the same metaphysical thought in Saint Thomas's celebration of being as the supreme attribute of divinity; and that for both Aristotle and Saint Thomas the concept of the unmoved mover is important in their way of conceiving the deity. The philosophical reader knows further that already in Plato there is a suggestion of the fantastic mythology of the soul's descent from oneness to the mortal state, which is a state of agitation, of change and decay, and which, while it is somehow necessary to the realization of the supreme One, yet involves for the souls that participate in it a kind of degradation. This notion, in Plato so poetical, and, as I have suggested, mythological, is taken up with great seriousness by Plotinus and other Neoplatonists, and through them it has passed over into English poetry and has left its dubious mark on much popular philosophic thinking. It is this high concept of the One and the Many, as I suppose, which has taken such a curious turn in More's "Definitions of Dualism" and given Babbitt his curious notion that the essence of good lies in the inhibition of natural impulse.

The poets, I may say, have done better justice to the subject. Our poets, from Spenser to Eliot, have made a clearer, a less confused, and a more human statement of the metaphysical problem of the One and the Many. And not least among them the ailing romantics — the grievously morbid Shelley and the more mildly infected Wordsworth. Let me relieve the tedium of our critical inquiry by quoting a sonnet of Wordsworth's not ungermane to this subject of the One and the Many, and so much more intelligible, so much more inspiring than the "Definitions of Dualism"! It is the final sonnet in the series on the River Duddon.

> I thought of Thee, my partner and my guide,
> As being past away. — Vain sympathies!
> For, backward, Duddon! as I cast my eyes,
> I see what was, and is, and will abide;
> Still glides the Stream, and shall for ever glide;
> The Form remains, the Function never dies;

While we, the brave, the mighty, and the wise,
We Men, who in our morn of youth defied
The elements, must vanish; — be it so!
Enough, if something from our hands have power
To live, and act, and serve the future hour;
And if, as toward the silent tomb we go,
Through love, through hope, and faith's
    transcendent dower,
We feel that we are greater than we know.

"We feel that we are greater than we know." Was anything profounder ever uttered by philosopher, any statement more moving ever framed by poet, on the subject of man's fate, "la condition humaine"? And how utterly romantic! How uncongenial to the taste of those whose stern motto is, "We know we should be stricter than we feel."

One sees in this sonnet of Wordsworth how much more is involved than the metaphysical problem of the One and the Many. More urgent than the metaphysical problem for the poet is the human condition suggested by Spenser's and Shelley's word, "mutability." Movement and action imply change, and change implies loss of identity, disintegration, decay, and death. It implies subjection to the laws of nature, to accident and circumstance, to suffering, infection, and all that threatens the integrity of the human spirit. This general theme has been largely treated by the English poets. Donne attacks it vigorously in his contrast between essential and accidental joys in his poem on the second anniversary of the death of Elizabeth Drury.

But pause, my soule; And study, ere thou fall
On accidentall joyes, th'essentiall.
Still before Accessories doe abide
A triall, must the principall be tride.
And what essentiall joy can'st thou expect
Here upon earth? what permanent effect
Of transitory causes? Dost thou love
Beauty? (And beauty worthy'st is to move)

> Poore cousened cousenor, *that* she, and *that* thou,
> Which did begin to love, are neither now;
> You are both fluid, chang'd since yesterday;
> Next day repaires, (but ill) last dayes decay.
> Nor are, (although the river keepe the name)
> Yesterdaies waters, and to daies the same.
> So flowes her face, and thine eyes, neither now
> That Saint, nor Pilgrime, which your loving vow
> Concern'd, remaines; but whil'st you thinke you bee
> Constant, you'are hourely in inconstancie.

The exemption from accident and change which cannot be had during life religious poets generally find in the region beyond death, that "undiscovered country" which has been so largely explored by the poetic imagination. Even Shelley, with the best will in the world to dispense with this fabled heaven, falls back, in his effort to represent a poet's immortality, on a Platonic or Neoplatonic counterpart of the Christian heaven. Incidentally, he has given perhaps the finest recital in English poetry of the sufferings and humiliations to which the spirit lies open in the mortal state.

> Peace, peace! he is not dead, he doth not sleep —
> He hath awakened from the dream of life —
> 'Tis we, who lost in stormy visions, keep
> With phantoms an unprofitable strife,
> And in mad trance, strike with our spirit's knife
> Invulnerable nothings. — *We* decay
> Like corpses in a charnel; fear and grief
> Convulse us and consume us day by day,
> And cold hopes swarm within our living clay.
>
> He has outsoared the shadow of our night;
> Envy and calumny and hate and pain,
> And that unrest which men miscall delight,
> Can touch him not and torture not again;
> From the contagion of the world's slow stain
> He is secure, and now can never mourn
> A heart grown cold, a head grown gray in vain;

Nor, when the spirit's self has ceased to burn,
With sparkless ashes load an unlamented urn.

The more stoical Arthur Clough eschews the "fairy-tale"
of heaven (to use Arnold's phrase) and contents himself
with the steadfastness of abstract truth, "with whom is no
variableness, neither shadow of turning."

> It fortifies my soul to know
> That, though I perish, Truth is so:
> That, howsoe'er I stray and range,
> Whate'er I do, Thou dost not change.
> I steadier step when I recall
> That, if I slip, Thou dost not fall.

But the keenest of contemporary poets returns to the
strict Catholic opposition of mortal and immortal, fortified
by something of metaphysics and by a great deal of penetrating if morbid psychology. Neglecting the ills that come
to us from outside, "envy and calumny and hate and pain,"
Eliot has given an analysis of "that unrest which men miscall
delight" — those ills which we make for ourselves through
heeding the voice of mortal ambition and desire, and the
withering of the spirit when it is realized that life in time
and the "actual" is not life in the "real" and eternal. This
disillusionment he describes in the opening movement of
his tone poem, or litany, upon Ash Wednesday. In the second movement he recites the hymn of his dead bones in
honor of the mystic Garden

> Where all loves end
> Terminate torment
> Of love unsatisfied
> The greater torment
> Of love satisfied
> End of the endless
> Journey to no end
> Conclusion of all
> That is inconclusible.

It is so that the poets give an infinitely more eloquent and plausible account than the humanist critics of our reasons for discontent with action and movement, and for cleaving instead to peace and steadfastness. Eliot is of them all the one who pursues this theme with the most burning iciness of psychological penetration. It is he who breathes the most desolating sense of the futility of all human endeavor — the self-defeat we inevitably court with every movement of mortal desire and ambition. Eliot has been a qualified disciple of Babbitt's school, and he suggests reasons not yet clearly formulated for the stress laid by the humanists upon their dogma of the inner check. He gives a very convincing account of why he and the humanists feel that they cannot drink "there, where trees flower, and springs flow." Only, he writes in terms of psychology, religion, and poetry, and they write in terms of a puritan morality.

What the humanists find most questionable in the romantic poets is a certain openness and expansiveness of heart. An open heart is one exposed too helplessly to the influences and suggestions of the natural world. And that is why these critics fall so furiously on Wordsworth's innocent recommendation of a "wise passiveness" to the gentle and peaceful influence of nature, and his bold poetic assertion that

> One impulse from a vernal wood
> May teach you more of man,
> Of moral evil and of good,
> Than all the sages can.

These critics do not take Wordsworth's statements in their context. They do not sufficiently consider that he is here opposing the heart as a source of inspiration to the mechanical reason of eighteenth-century philosophy — that in all probability he is in the very process of freeing himself from the thrall of Godwin, than whom they could surely hold no thinker more in abhorrence. They do not realize that "heart" is the poetic term which most nearly corresponds to philosophical intuition, and that as such it had been opposed to reason in the famous epigram of the religious Pascal, "Le coeur a ses raisons que la raison ne connaît pas." They do not consider how many seventeenth-century implications cling to the word "nature" as Wordsworth employs it — that for him, as for Cicero and Henry More, nature may be the mother of that "right reason" which is the direct intuitive knowledge of right and wrong. They cannot conceive the romantic daring with which Wordsworth associates nature in that sense with nature as it comprises Mother Earth, with all her vernal woods. If they could conceive it, they would condemn it as a sophistical trick of the devil, naturalism. But apart from the poet's unwarranted association of nature as wisdom with nature as scenery, they cannot afford to admit the legitimacy of the concept of nature as wisdom. Their dualism is strict and absolute. They admit but one meaning for one word, though their own meaning may be an unstable composite. What they mean by a word the romantics must mean; they must mean the same thing every time they use it; and they are liable to prosecution if, on the basis of this meaning, the text is open to dangerous interpretations. Thus critics are caught in semantic traps, and poets are held for damages.

Poetry as Recapitulation

"GAINING AS WE GIVE
THE LIFE WE IMAGE"

THUS far I have briefly outlined the More and Babbitt dualism of movement and stillness and their great dogma of the inner check, and by references to Plato and citations from the poets have shown how these doctrines might be given a very real human significance. But I have not yet done justice to the humanists' distrust of expansiveness of the spirit. This they find to be the great weakness of the romantics. What they evidently feel is that the open heart is a heart exposed to the temptations of the flesh; that what passes for sentiment in the romantics is too often a mere disguise for appetite, and that the soul thus subject to the assaults of appetite is one that has lost command of itself. It is in the interest of the stoic ideal of self-possession, self-command, that they deprecate the romantic subjection to impulse.

That, at least, is the best light in which I can set their doctrine. Only, so far as I know, they give no such account of the satisfactions of self-command as Epictetus or Marcus Aurelius gives. And, of course, their dualism is differently drawn. They locate the cleft in our nature on an imaginary line between the natural and the human, whereas the stoics locate it between brute nature (the region of necessity) and that nature which we share with the divine, whose impulses are good. In stoicism self-command is a relatively bright and gladsome state; in Babbitt it has the air of a sterile discipline. It is Marcus Aurelius rendered by Cotton Mather or Jonathan Edwards, only of course without benefit of heaven and hell.

Babbitt's references to the infinite cravings of the romantic soul remind me sometimes of Carlyle, not in the tone, which is similar only in its austerity, but in the like notion of insatiable appetite. Says Teufelsdröckh:

Man's Unhappiness, as I construe, comes of his Greatness; it is because there is an Infinite in him, which with all his cunning he cannot quite bury under the Finite. Will the whole Finance Ministers and Upholsterers and Confectioners of Modern Europe undertake, in jointstock company, to make one Shoeblack HAPPY? They cannot accomplish it, above an hour or two; for the Shoeblack also has a soul quite other than his Stomach; and would require, if you consider it, for his permanent satisfaction and saturation, simply this allotment, no more, and no less: *God's infinite Universe altogether to himself,* therein to enjoy infinitely, and fill every wish as fast as it rose. Oceans of Hochheimer, a Throat like that of Ophiuchus: speak not of them; to the infinite Shoeblack they are as nothing. No sooner is your ocean filled, than he grumbles that it might have been of better vintage. Try him with half of a Universe, of an Omnipotence, he sets to quarrelling with the proprietor of the other half, and declares himself the most maltreated of men. — Always there is a black spot in our sunshine: it is even as I said, the *Shadow of Ourselves.*

I sometimes wonder whether in his youth Babbitt may not have read this or some similar passage in Carlyle, and, being deeply impressed with the notion of an infinite appetite, have carried it over into his doctrine, even after he had conceived his distaste for all romanticism, so that he could not possibly have found man's greatness in any such questionable infinite. Such are the devious ways of thought in its passage from mind to mind, from age to age. Perhaps no idea is ever launched on the gusty currents of world thought but it promptly passes through a dozen transformations and disguises. The student of the history of ideas — your Lovejoy or your Boas — has occasion every day, in the presence of some monstrous mask, to recognize a comely friend transmogrified, and so cry out with Quince: "Bless thee, Bottom! bless thee! thou art translated."

For Carlyle, the classic example of the infinite Shoeblack is the poet Byron, who was forever whining about the happiness that was denied him; the classic example of his opposite was Goethe, with his gospel of renunciation (*Entsagen*). And Teufelsdröckh's advice to himself is to "Close thy *Byron;* open thy *Goethe.*"

"*Es leuchtet mir ein,*" (he cried) "I see a glimpse of it! . . . there is in man a HIGHER than Love of Happiness: he can do without Happiness, and instead thereof find Blessedness! Was it not to preach forth this same HIGHER that sages and martyrs, the Poet and the Priest, in all times, have spoken and suffered; bearing testimony, through life and through death, of the Godlike that is in Man, and how in the Godlike only has he Strength and Freedom? Which God-inspired Doctrine art thou also honoured to be taught; O Heavens! and broken with manifold merciful Afflictions, even till thou become contrite, and learn it! O, thank thy Destiny for these; thankfully bear what yet remain: thou hadst need of them; the Self in thee needed to be annihilated. By benignant fever-paroxysms is Life rooting out the deep-seated chronic Disease, and triumphs over Death. On the roaring billows of Time, thou art not engulfed, but borne aloft into the azure of Eternity. Love not Pleasure; love God. This is the EVERLASTING YEA, wherein all contradiction is solved: wherein whoso walks and works, it is well with him."

Carlyle certainly gives a very free translation of Goethe's thought. Self-realization is surely a more characteristic doctrine with Goethe than self-annihilation; and if he recommended renunciation in one direction, it was only in favor of fulfillment in another — renunciation of a small part, fulfillment in the whole. What is most like him is the doctrine of the Godlike, though the features of godhood are better delineated elsewhere. The finest statement of Goethe's position in this matter is in his own "Das Göttliche," from which noble poem I shall quote forthwith certain passages, with a literal translation.

Das Göttliche

Edel sey der Mensch,
Hülfreich und gut!
Denn das allein
Unterscheidet ihn
Von allen Wesen,
Die wir kennen.
. . . .

Let man be noble, helpful and good! For that alone distinguishes him from all beings of which we have knowledge.
. . . .

Denn unfühlend
Ist die Natur:
Es leuchtet die Sonne
Ueber Bös' und Gute,
Und dem Verbrecher
Glänzen, wie dem Besten,
Der Mond und die Sterne.
. . . .

For unfeeling is nature: the sun illumines good and bad, and the moon and the stars shine upon the guilty as upon the best of men.
. . . .

Nach ewigen, ehrnen,
Grossen Gesetzen
Müssen wir alle
Unseres Daseyns
Kreise vollenden.

According to great eternal iron laws must we all fulfil the cycle of our being.

Nur allein der Mensch
Vermag das Unmögliche;
Er unterscheidet,
Wählet und richtet;
Er kann dem Augenblick
Dauer verleihen.

Man alone can perform the impossible; he makes distinctions, chooses and judges; he can give duration to the passing moment.

Er allein darf
Den Guten lohnen,
Den Bösen strafen,
Heilen und retten,
Alles Irrende, Schweifende
Nützlich verbinden.

He alone has power to reward the good, punish the evil, heal and save, and bind up featly all that is astray and at loose ends.

Here again is the One and the Many and the problem of mutability. By choosing and judging man can give essential permanence to the passing moment. And by good works he teaches us what to think of the gods. How simple and positive a system of ethics! Nothing of the inner check.

The strongest point in Babbitt's position, as I see it, is his determination not to confuse the issues with terminology drawn from religion. His philosophy is one that can be espoused by the unbeliever as well as by the Christian. That higher in man than love of happiness he does not call the Godlike but simply and boldly the human. I suppose that was one reason for his wide appeal in an age in which the concept of deity had taken on so much vagueness and uncertainty. Babbitt made a bold and earnest effort to set up a moral philosophy which should be secular; and that I admire in him. What keeps down my enthusiasm is the puritan and negative terms in which he defines this higher humanity. In this Carlyle and Goethe more than win back the advantage over him.

Since I am dealing so boldly in fancied influences, I can even imagine that I find in the moral dualism of More and Babbitt an echo of Carlyle's version of Kant's doctrine of free will. In so far as we are passively subject to the operations of phenomena, according to Kant, we are a part of nature and slaves of necessity. But whenever we set about deliberately to act, we are moving in another dimension, and are conscious of ourselves as free agents. In Kant, too, there is a close association between sensual desire and subjection to necessity. So that the stage is all set for Carlyle's opposition between eating (symbol of sensuality) and working (symbol of voluntary action), and the solution of the problem of freedom he draws from this opposition.

"TEMPTATIONS in the Wilderness!" exclaims Teufelsdröckh: "Have we not all to be tried with such? Not so easily can the old

Adam, lodged in us by birth, be dispossessed. Our Life is com- passed round with Necessity; yet is the meaning of Life itself no other than Freedom, than Voluntary Force: thus have we a warfare; in the beginning, especially, a hard-fought battle. For the God-given mandate, *Work thou in Welldoing*, lies mysteri- ously written, in Promethean Prophetic Characters, in our hearts; and leaves us no rest, night or day, till it be deciphered and obeyed; till it burn forth, in our conduct, a visible, acted Gospel of Freedom. And as the clay-given mandate, *Eat thou and be filled*, at the same time persuasively proclaims itself through every nerve, — must there not be a confusion, a contest, before the better Influence can become the upper?"

So then, in Carlyle, the thing reduces itself to a choice be- tween hedonistic self-indulgence and beneficent activity. If we yield supinely to self-indulgence, we are the slaves of our appetites and are doomed to perpetual disappointment and misery. It is by positive action that we free ourselves from the dominance of necessity.

Whether Carlyle has succeeded in solving the philosoph- ical problem of freedom and necessity where so many have failed, I will leave to better heads to determine. He has surely met in a highly suggestive manner what we may call the problem of *ethical* freedom; he has offered a sound and inspiring rule for meeting life with force and dignity. What is decadent and self-destructive in Epicureanism he displaces with something positive and challenging to the active spirit. The weakness of Babbitt's moral system is, as I have said, its negative character. For the attractions of natural impulse he has offered no substitute but the sterile complacencies of self-command.

The weakness of this point of view is well hit off by Matthew Arnold in his famous opposition of Hellenism and Hebraism. "The governing idea of Hellenism," Arnold says, "is *spontaneity of consciousness;* that of Hebraism, *strict- ness of conscience.*" Now, spontaneity of consciousness is exactly what Babbitt distrusts in literature; strictness of conscience precisely what governs him in his doctrine of the inner check. He wants us to check our impulses, in the last analysis, because he is ridden with the idea of sin. That is not what he calls it, for he wishes to give his work a secular and worldly tone. But that is what it amounts to. And we are reminded of Arnold's penetrating account of Hebraism as an obsession with sin.

Under the name of sin, the difficulties of knowing oneself and conquering oneself which impede man's passage to perfection, become, for Hebraism, a positive, active entity hostile to man, a mysterious power which I heard Dr. Pusey the other day, in one of his impressive sermons, compare to a hideous hunchback seated on our shoulders, and which it is the main business of our lives to hate and oppose. The discipline of the Old Testament may be summed up as a discipline teaching us to abhor and flee from sin; the discipline of the New Testament, as a discipline teaching us to die to it. As Hellenism speaks of thinking clearly, seeing things in their essence and beauty, as a grand and precious feat for man to achieve, so Hebraism speaks of becoming conscious of sin, of wakening to a sense of sin, as a feat of this kind. It is obvious to what wide divergence these differing tendencies, actively followed, must lead. As one passes and repasses from Hellenism to Hebraism, from Plato to St. Paul, one feels inclined to rub one's eyes and ask oneself whether man is indeed a gentle and simple being, showing the traces of a noble and divine nature; or an unhappy chained captive, labouring with groanings that cannot be uttered to free himself from the body of this death.

We know what great importance Arnold ascribes to Hebraism as a primary check on the movements of our gross animality. We also know that he considers this side of our moral life to have been comparatively well provided for in the England of his day and for the most part in Europe since the time of the Reformation. Ever since the Renaissance, as Arnold thinks, the central current of the world's progress has been in the line of Hellenism. There have been cross-currents of Hebraism, and "the cross and the check have been necessary and salutary."

But that does not do away with the essential difference between the main stream of man's advance and a cross or a side stream. For more than two hundred years the main stream of man's advance has moved towards knowing himself and the world, seeing things as they are, spontaneity of consciousness; the main impulse of a great part, and that the strongest part, of our nation has been towards strictness of conscience. They have made the secondary the principal at the wrong moment, and the principal they have at the wrong moment treated as secondary. This contravention of the natural order has produced, as such contravention always must produce, a certain confusion and false movement, of which we are now beginning to feel, in almost every direction, the inconvenience.

Thus far I have been speaking of Babbitt's system as an ethical system and its inadequacy as such. It seems to me to leave out what forms the starting point and cornerstone of all the great ethical systems — some positive ideal of good, with some notion of the goods which flow to mankind from that ideal. I do not believe you can base a sound ethical system on mere prohibitions and inhibitions. These are of course a necessary part of our practical equipment if we are to get anywhere in our personal or our social life. They are necessary in ethics as they are in the civil code. They are useful as the police are useful. Some prohibitions are necessary in the discipline of children, as a means of starting good habits and promoting order in family life. But an exclusive diet of prohibitions in childhood will hardly give you anything better than criminals and eunuchs. The creature will turn upon a society that gives him nothing better to live for; or a life that might be so rich and useful will be reduced to guarding the pasha's treasure and his harem. I speak simply and in the terms of traditional common sense.

If you turn to psychology, to any one of the seven schools, they will give you in horrifying detail the effects of building a life on the inner check.

But what we are directly concerned with here is the bearing of Babbitt's system on esthetics, on the making and enjoyment of poetry. With my notion of the nature of poetry and its essential office in helping us realize the quality of our life, I naturally cannot accept an esthetic that is grounded in nothing better than the sense of order and would secure order by the simple expedient of inhibiting impulses. What it amounts to is little less than saying *no* to the operations of the human spirit. Now, the operations of the human spirit are, we need to consider, extremely various, subtle, obscure, and of almost inconceivable force. To say no to them is a hazardous and dubious business. It is like sealing up the springs. . . . And who would wish to seal up the springs? Whoever notes that a spring comes from the earth and that earth is evil.

Babbitt's dichotomy of human nature makes me think of Ruskin's dichotomy of plant life. In one of his letters to workingmen Ruskin was taking exception to the theory of some lecturer on botany that all the members of a plant are interchangeable, or, as Ruskin reports it, that petals are really leaves and there is no such thing as a flower. Ruskin cites this pronouncement with horror and scorn as an example of the general temper of modern science. "It gives lectures on Botany," he says, "of which the object is to show that there is no such thing as a flower; on Humanity, to show that there is no such thing as a Man; on Theology, to show there is no such thing as a God." Now, that is a right witty statement of the reaction of a man like Ruskin to, let us say, the ideas of a man like Huxley. But very shortly Ruskin's wit gives way to an exhibition of Victorian baby talk that must absolutely take the prize.

I must explain the real meaning to you, however, of that saying of the Botanical lecturer, for it has a wide bearing. Some fifty years ago, the poet Goethe discovered that all the parts of plants had a kind of common nature, and would change into each other. Now this was a true discovery, and a notable one; and you will find that, in fact, all plants are composed of essentially two parts — the leaf and root — one loving the light, the other darkness; one liking to be clean, the other to be dirty; one liking to grow for the most part up, the other for the most part down; and each having faculties and purposes of its own. But the pure one which loves the light has, above all things, the purpose of being married to another leaf, and having child-leaves, and children's children of leaves, to make the earth fair forever. And when the leaves marry, they put on wedding-robes, and are more glorious than Solomon in all his glory, and they have feasts of honey, and we call them "Flowers."

All that is wanting is a surpliced bishop and the Mendelssohn wedding march. The bridal flowers are furnished by the contracting parties.

Well, Ruskin was too good a botanist to wish to exclude the roots from participation in the economy of plant life, even though they be dirty and dark-loving members. And I distrust any philosopher who proposes to cut man off from his roots because they grow for the most part down, or who would seal up the springs of the spirit because they flow out of the earth. The project is to seal up the springs and set out pails to catch the water that falls from the sky. It will be softer water, anyway, and free from the taste of minerals that clings to the waters under the earth. But do not think for a moment that the subterranean waters will be so easily confined. You cannot say no to the law of gravity. You may have sealed up the spring on the hillside; but the next thing it will be gushing up in the basement and wash away the house.

But the loss of a house is a minor inconvenience. One can always set to work again and erect another habitation. The greater danger is the total deprivation of drinking water. Suppose your stream can find some other way to the level it seeks and flow, like Alph the sacred river, through caverns measureless to man, down to a sunless sea. We know the kind of desert land of which such rivers are the feature, with the parched winds blowing over wastes of sand where no green thing can root. It is literally life — the life of the spirit — which is at stake when it is proposed to say no to the creative impulse of the poetic imagination.

My notion of poetry as a form of living is familiar to the poets. Perhaps the finest expression of the idea is found in Byron.

> 'Tis to create, and in creating live
> A being more intense, that we endow
> With form our fancy, gaining as we give
> The life we image, even as I do now.
> What am I? Nothing: but not so art thou,
> Soul of my thought! with whom I traverse earth,
> Invisible but gazing, as I glow
> Mix'd with thy spirit, blended with thy birth,
> And feeling still with thee in my crush'd feelings'
>   dearth.

Ah, but Byron's statement plunges us at once into complications for which we are not yet prepared. It suits our theme well in that it lays the emphasis on living as the object of poetic activity on the identity of the two forms of activity.

> 'Tis to create, and in creating live
> A being more intense, that we endow
> With form our fancy, gaining as we give
> The life we image, even as I do now.

But this brings in the new criterion of intensity, which might well demand our attention. There are many things to be desiderated in living, and intensity is perhaps not the most important. Refinement of quality, elevation of tone are other things that may be desired, and by poets of a certain temperament much to be preferred to mere intensity. To such as these the very term "intensity" may be a trifle suspect, as carrying with it a suggestion of violence or unbalance of feeling.

But this is something we cannot stop to discuss. What is more pressing is Byron's suggestion that the life he seeks in his imaginative activity is not the life he lives in his private capacity; that what he creates will be not so much a statement, a recapitulation, of his own personal experience as another form of living to take its place.

> What am I? Nothing: but not so art thou,
> Soul of my thought! with whom I traverse earth,
> Invisible but gazing, as I glow
> Mix'd with thy spirit, blended with thy birth,
> And feeling still with thee in my crush'd feelings'
> dearth.

This passage occurs early in the third canto of "Childe Harold's Pilgrimage." Byron had just passed through a period marked by his first great literary triumphs and by the most harrowing experiences of his personal life. He had waked on a morning to find himself famous. Walter Scott's mantle had fallen on his shoulders. He had been for a season the lion of London society.

He has now made his curious blundering try at marital happiness, and found himself in an impasse of irreconcilable temperaments. He has been the victim of his own morbid and perverse nature. He has been separated from wife and child; has become the subject of general obloquy both for his personal conduct and his political opinions. He goes abroad into virtual exile. He takes up again his interrupted pilgrimage. He feels himself to be personally null. But he still has his creative imagination. He still has the soul of his thought in which he may live an intense and glowing life. He will live not in his individual concerns, but in the thought of what is loveliest and noblest and most dramatic in the scenery and history of the lands he visits.

He visits the battlefield of Waterloo, and meditates on the death of patriots and on the riddle of Bonaparte's character. He visits Morat and sings of Marathon and the heroic struggle for freedom. He visits Lake Geneva; he meditates on the characters of Rousseau, Voltaire, and Gibbon. (His thoughts on historical characters, by the way, are as conventional and moral in substance as we might expect from a Presbyterian minister, though much more musical, and cast in terms that almost invariably escape banality and often verge upon the sublime.) On Lake Geneva the mountains and the stars inspire him with large religious thoughts, in a vein he might have drawn from Wordsworth, but uttered in his own more resonant voice. At length he comes to Italy, and there his soul can expand in the thought of greatness passed away and of freedom taking root in the wilderness of Columbia, or even persisting desperately in Albion.

> Yet, Freedom, yet thy banner, torn but flying,
> Streams like the thunder-storm *against* the wind;
> Thy trumpet voice, though broken now and dying,
> The loudest still the tempest leaves behind:
> Thy tree has lost its blossoms, and the rind,
> Chopp'd by the axe, looks rough and little worth,
> But the sap lasts, — and still the seed we find
> Sown deep, even in the bosom of the North;
> So shall a better Spring less bitter fruit bring forth.

Venice enchants him, even in its slavish state, because of the beauty that has survived its glory, and especially because of the memory of Tasso and the immortality given to the place by the art of Otway, Radcliffe, Schiller, Shakespeare. These, with the creatures of their imagination, would

repeople the shores of Venice though no citizens remained.
For —

> The beings of the mind are not of clay;
> Essentially immortal, they create
> And multiply in us a brighter ray
> And more beloved existence. That which Fate
> Prohibits to dull life, in this our state
> Of mortal bondage, by these spirits supplied,
> First exiles, then replaces what we hate;
> Watering the heart whose early flowers have died,
> And with a fresher growth replenishing the void.

The case of Byron, and that of "Childe Harold," is much more complex than I have indicated. There is a personal theme running through these later cantos of the poem that would require patient study to determine its bearing on our problem. But I have given a sufficient account of the topics from history and nature which form the overt subject matter; and enough to suggest in a preliminary way this particular function of poetry, by which, to use Byron's word, it is made to *replace* what is hateful in personal experience with a form of living more satisfying.

> That which Fate
> Prohibits to dull life, in this our state
> Of mortal bondage, by these spirits supplied,
> First exiles, then replaces what we hate.

Perhaps we might find in Byron, too, examples of the simpler process of restatement, or recapitulation, of what has been satisfying in itself. But much better examples may be found elsewhere. Among the best would be those epic and heroic poems in which the poet rehearses for his tribe the noble deeds of their ancestors — poems like the "Iliad," the "Beowulf," the "Chanson de Roland." We can imagine the countless occasions on which the group of earls and thanes assembled in the great hall have listened to this recital of deeds which, though distant in time and distinctly ideal-ized, must seem to them hardly more than their own deeds — or, at any rate, a glorified version of their own way of life.

It is true that the gods no longer interposed so often in the affairs of men, and one was not so likely to meet in com-bat laughter-loving Aphrodite or Ares, blood-stained bane of mortals. But still the gods were worshipped and propi-tiated; still they had their favorites. The strength of men had declined since the time of Diomedes, who alone could wield a stone "such as two men, as men now are, would not avail to lift." But strength was still strength and courage courage, and there were still warriors pre-eminent over others as Hector and Achilles were pre-eminent. Wisdom in council was now as precious and as rare, and eloquent speaking as effective. The enemies were no longer horse-taming Tro-jans, nor the field of battle the Skamandrian plain. But still there was desperate fighting in mountain passes and upon the plains of Hellas. The Achaians still were mail-clad and glancing-eyed. Oaths were oaths and sacred, though often violated. Honor was honor, and the godlike beauty of women was still a power for good and evil.

But while the hearts of the hearers swelled with the thought of deeds and gestures which might well be their own, it was perhaps in the homelier features of daily life that the plain citizen most recognized the very countenance of things — in the familiar arrangements and procedures of domestic economy, and above all in the play of the ele-ments, in beasts and birds, and whatever affected his flocks and vineyards. The Greeks lived by the rocky shores or at the foot of mountains, or both. They were well acquainted with the ways of wind and wave.

So spake he, and the Argives shouted aloud, like to a wave on a steep shore, when the south wind cometh and stirreth it; even on a jutting rock, that is never left at peace by the waves of all winds that rise from this side and from that. And they stood up and scattered in haste throughout the ships, and made fires in the huts and took their meal.

Well they knew the dangers of mist to the shepherd.

Even as when the south wind sheddeth mist over the crests of a mountain, mist unwelcome to the shepherd, but to the robber better than night, and a man can see no further than he casteth a stone; even so thick arose the gathering dust-clouds at their tread as they went; and with all speed they advanced across the plain.

With the ways of beasts wild and tame they were intimately familiar.

And as the many tribes of feathered birds, wild geese or cranes or long-necked swans, on the Asian mead by Kaystrios' stream, fly hither and thither joying in their plumage, and with loud cries settle ever onwards, and the mead resounds; even so poured forth the many tribes of warriors from ships and huts into the Skamandrian plain. And the earth echoed terribly beneath the tread of men and horses. So stood they in the flowery Skamandrian plain, unnumbered as are leaves and flowers in their season. Even as the many tribes of thick flies that hover about a herdsman's steading in the spring season, when milk drencheth the pails, even in like number stood the flowing-haired Achaians upon the plain in the face of the Trojans, eager to rend them asunder. And even as the goatherds easily divide the ranging flocks of goats when they mingle in the pasture, so did their captains marshall them on this side and on that, to enter into the fray, and in their midst lord Agamemnon, his head and eyes like unto Zeus whose joy is in the thunder, and his waist like unto Ares and his breast unto Poseidon. Even as a bull standeth out far foremost amid the herd, for he is pre-eminent amid the pasturing kine, even such did Zeus make Atreides that day, pre-eminent among many and chief amid heroes.

In the epic version of things, one is impressed above all with the marrowy zest and jubilancy that runs through the record from beginning to end and shows forth in every least detail. All is song and exultation. And it does not require the hexameters nor even the bright tongue of the original to make one feel this shining quality. One is strongly conscious of it in a good translation, like this of Lang, Leaf, and Myers, which, with a fine English prose rhythm, faithfully preserves the essentials of imagery and diction and those conventional narrative devices that give a constant elevation of tone.

One such device is the regular varying of act with speech. Nothing can be got done in this world of noble doing without the aid of talk — the taking of counsel, debate and intrigue, the wiles of deception or the honest rhetoric of persuasion. This is admirable, of course, as a mere device of storytelling. It serves to complicate the plot, works up suspense, builds up imaginatively to the moments of action, relieves the tenseness, and diversifies the narrative. But more than this, it is a means of raising the tone. For it adds the nobility of spoken sentiment to that inherent in the action, and to sentiment it lends all the stateliness and dignity of high rhetoric. It adds to the deed the potent magic of the word.

To this convention of substance is joined the minor stylistic convention of following every speech with the formal statement, "so spake he." "So spake the hero and persuaded his brother's heart with just counsel; and he obeyed." "So spake she, and the bright-eyed goddess Athene disregarded not; but went darting down from the peaks of Olympus, and came with speed to the fleet ships of the Achaians." This might seem a naive way of making transition to the following incident; it might be expected to grow monotonous. And indeed it would be monotonous, and worse, if the phrase were something more pretentious and if it did not render so well the delight of the poet in words well spoken and of high sentence. As it is, the phrase is no more monotonous than a flourish of trumpets to announce the king or the sounding of a bugle for lowering the flag.

More elaborate is the epic simile, but it certainly does not grow monotonous as used by Homer. The comparisons are infinitely varied, fresh and vivid, and drawn so clearly from observation that they lend a special kind of animation to the whole. Some of them deal with the mighty and awe-inspiring aspects of nature, and these are suited to the grandeur of the main action. Others bring in the homelier details of natural history and pastoral life, and, without lowering the tone, yet relieve the effect of the heroic and legendary, supporting these with a realism drawn from common life. For the Greeks of Homer's time they must have made the action more convincing; and for us they help provide a general imaginative setting for the story. They are as decorative as a running frieze of natural forms. And in their regular recurrence they are like motives in music, and contribute to the larger rhythm of movement and theme, which is as essential to poetry as the metrical rhythm of the line.

The poet delights in everything that comes within the range of his comment; in the splendor of the gods, their swiftness and beauty of movement, their supernatural powers, and their so human passions. He delights in the turn of fate by which the coward goddess Aphrodite was wounded in combat by the mortal Diomedes, and immortal blood flowed from the goddess's white arms; in the chaffing that she had at the hands of Athene, and the smiling advice she received from the father of gods. "Not unto thee, my child, are given the works of war; but follow thou after the loving tasks of wedlock, and to all these things shall fleet Ares and Athene look."

The poet exults in all that pertains to his warriors, be they Trojans or Achaians — their godlike beauty and manliness of figure; their passions, so like the gods', and ready and right response to every cause of emotion — to grief and anger and hurt pride — their loyalty to friend and chief, their courage and craftiness and Yankee ingenuity. He is delighted with such romantic turns as that which brings together in mortal combat Diomedes the Greek and Glaukos, glorious son of Lykian Hippolochos, when the obligation to fight the enemy gives way to the obligation to spare the guest-friend of one's father. There is something in the prowess of the Trojan adversary that leads Diomedes to ask him who he may be; and when Glaukos proudly recites the names and qualities of his sire and grandsire, the son of Tydeus recalls that his grandfather had entertained the grandfather of Glaukos in Argos, and they had exchanged goodly gifts of friendship.

Oineus gave a belt bright with purple, and Bellerophon a gold two-handled cup. Therefore now am I to thee a dear guest-friend in midmost Argos, and thou in Lykia, whene'er I fare to your land. So let us shun each other's spears, even amid the throng; Trojans are there in multitudes and famous allies for me to slay . . . and for thee are there Achaians in multitude. . . . But let us make exchange of arms between us, that these also may know how we avow ourselves to be guest-friends by lineage."
    So spake the twain, and leaping from their cars clasped each the other by his hand, and pledged their faith.

It was a mighty touching episode and heartening reminder of bonds of friendship that reach across the barriers of race and nation. But noble and right as was the impulse on one side and the other, the poet cannot forbear to note that Diomedes' proposal for an exchange of armor was not quite sporting under the circumstances, and that Glaukos's acceptance of it was indicative of a worldly shrewdness somewhat under the Hellenic standard. "But now Zeus son of Kronos took from Glaukos his wits, in that he made exchange with Diomedes Tydeus' son of golden armour for bronze, the price of five score oxen for the price of nine."

With such a relish for both high and low does Homer record the incidents of heroic life. And because there is a predominance of the high — because, as we say, the subject is idealized — we must not hastily conclude that it is consciously falsified, that the poet is not giving a proper "imitation of nature," or that to the hearer of these songs they do not convey the sense of truth. Epic idealization is three parts selection and emphasis and one part exaggeration. I know not by what fractional part of one per cent to reckon the element of sheer distortion. As for selection, emphasis, and exaggeration, these are the natural accompaniments to any enthusiastic account of experience. Idealization is simply the representation of life as it appears to us in the moments when we take most satisfaction in it. It is a normal process of the mind when it has not yielded to despondency or girt itself up to the strenuous tasks of critical and scientific statement. And the epic style is doubtless the one most natural to a people in presenting its history.

Recapitulation in the Lyric

IN the last chapter I gave some illustration of how, in epic poetry, the people may rejoice together in the exploits of their forebears. The people is an august and mighty thing, and it is perhaps easier for an individual to take pride in the exploits of his race or tribe than in his own. Still, there is store of lyric poems in which the author expresses satisfaction in experiences personal to him, to which the reader will respond as an individual in so far as the poet's words remind him of similar experiences or imaginatively induce them in him for the first time. Shall we take for an example Wordsworth's famous sonnet "Composed upon Westminster Bridge"?

> Earth has not anything to show more fair:
> Dull would he be of soul who could pass by
> A sight so touching in its majesty:
> This City now doth, like a garment, wear
> The beauty of the morning; silent, bare,
> Ships, towers, domes, theatres, and temples lie
> Open unto the fields, and to the sky;
> All bright and glittering in the smokeless air.
> Never did sun more beautifully steep
> In his first splendour, valley, rock, or hill;
> Ne'er saw I, never felt, a calm so deep!
> The river glideth at his own sweet will:
> Dear God! the very houses seem asleep;
> And all that mighty heart is lying still!

This poem is beautiful enough without comment, for the mere visual picture of a city lying steeped in the sun's first splendor, like some lovely creature not yet wakened from sleep. But I think it gains greatly by consideration of the lifelong sentiments of Wordsworth in regard to cities and in particular the city of London. Many a present-day reader has wondered, no doubt, where one can obtain a single comprehensive view of London worthy of such ecstatic admiration, or of London lying "open unto the fields and to the sky." London is no Florence, no Venice, no Carcassonne, to be taken in at a glance and seen as a part of nature. And readers accustomed to think of Wordsworth as primarily a nature poet might even be surprised to find him celebrating this crowded warren of vice and sophistication with as much warmth and tenderness as if it were some secluded valley among the Cumberland hills.

Well, to begin with, whatever the views of critics, and however well they may be justified by the relative success of his poems dealing with nature and with man, Wordsworth, among his many references to himself, never, I believe, spoke of himself as primarily a poet of external nature, but ever coupled nature with man as his closely related subjects. Sometimes, even where external nature is an important adjunct to his subject, as in "Michael," the theme is announced simply as "man, the heart of man, and human life." And then, with regard to cities, while it is true that they often plagued him with their dreary want of beauty —

> The close and overcrowded haunts
> Of cities, where the heart is sick,
> And the eye feeds it not, and cannot feed —

and while he was saddened there by the sight of vice and destitution in extreme and concentrated form, it is also true that he found in equal concentration reminders of the greatness of man's accomplishments enshrined in record and tradition, as well as evidence of that spiritual community which makes the abiding greatness of human society. As he has it in "The Prelude":

>   a sense
>   Of what in the Great City had been done
>   And suffered, and was doing, suffering, still,
>   Weighed with me, could support the test of thought;
>   And, in despite of all that had gone by,
>   Or was departing never to return,
>   There I conversed with majesty and power
>   Like independent natures.

And again:

>   Add also, that among the multitudes
>   Of that huge city, oftentimes was seen
>   Affectingly set forth, more than elsewhere
>   Is possible, the unity of man,
>   One spirit over ignorance and vice
>   Predominant, in good and evil hearts;
>   One sense for moral judgments, as one eye
>   For the sun's light.

Then furthermore, the sight of urban misery and vice was a sharp challenge to him and his guiding "trust in what we may become." And this moral ideal and conviction shone all the brighter by contrast with what actually lay before his eyes.

>   Lo! everything that was indeed divine
>   Retained its purity inviolate,
>   Nay brighter shone, by this portentous gloom
>   Set off.

Still, we must observe that, in his London days, the thought of natural beauty among the wilds was a constant solace and refreshment to an eye and heart so wearied by what they must perforce take in. And—

>   Oft, in lonely rooms, and 'mid the din
>   Of towns and cities, I have owed to them,
>   In hours of weariness, sensations sweet,
>   Felt in the blood, and felt along the heart;
>   And passing even into my purer mind,
>   With tranquil restoration.

The Hawkshead boy must have suffered much from home-sickness in the stony wastes of London, and the reverie of Poor Susan is doubtless the reproduction of many a mood of his own. For him as for her, the morning song of a thrush at a street corner is a "note of enchantment," and he sees

> A mountain ascending, a vision of trees;
> Bright volumes of vapour through Lothbury glide,
> And a river flows on through the vale of Cheapside.

When he wishes to give adequate expression to the majesty and power of man's past deeds, he must render them in terms of the spirit he has felt as moving in external nature; and the city

> Was thronged with impregnations like the wilds.

And so when he has his vision of the city clothed with the beauty of the morning, the highest tribute he can pay to it as an object of esthetic contemplation is this:

> Never did sun more beautifully steep
> In his first splendour, valley, rock, or hill.

That was before the age of steam and universal coal smoke, and before the vast enlargement of population. Wordsworth could actually see his city

> Open unto the fields, and to the sky.

And if he was to see it as supremely beautiful he must thus view it in the framework of nature.

But it was still the crowded haunts of men that was the subject of his picture, the life of the city in all its various aspects, — commerce, politics, art, and religion — ships, towers, domes, theaters, and temples. He saw it in its monumental character as record and witness

> Of what in the Great City had been done
> And suffered, and was doing, suffering, still.

He saw it as the visible symbol of human society —

> the unity of man,
> One spirit over ignorance and vice
> Predominant, in good and evil hearts;
> One sense for moral judgments, as one eye
> For the sun's light.

And he saw it as a heart not yet awakened to the heat and turmoil of its daily life.

> Ne'er saw I, never felt, a calm so deep!
> The river glideth at his own sweet will:
> Dear God! the very houses seem asleep;
> And all that mighty heart is lying still!

No one is more in love with stillness and calmness than this romantic poet. No one has more frequent and more affecting figures drawn from sleep. According to him, the office of a poet is to reap

> The harvest of a quiet eye
> That broods and sleeps on his own heart.

In our moments of most penetrating vision, he says,

> the breath of this corporeal frame
> And even the motion of our human blood
> Almost suspended, we are laid asleep
> In body, and become a living soul.

In one of the loveliest and most quietly insinuating of his characterizations of inanimate things, he speaks, in a single line, of

> Waters running, falling, or asleep.

Wordsworth is certainly not the man to find in the staying of impulse the very center and definition of the moral life, though he is full enough of recommendations for the staying of impulses noxious or out of season. He is not one to erect stillness or calm into the final word for moral greatness, or to place life's supreme value in the cessation of movement and the transcending of all diversity. Like other fine poets, he celebrates activity and peace, diversity and oneness, as the eternal poles of living experience, between which the heart moves in constant, regular alternation. Like all great actors and composers he knows the value of the rest, the nicely calculated pause, to let the beauty of the thing sink in. Now, the composer knows that the soul of music is movement, the actor knows that the life of the stage is action. But, still, it is in the moment of pause that confusion clears away and we apprehend things in the large, in their oneness; we suck the very marrow of the subject. So Wordsworth, in his sonnet composed on Westminster Bridge.

But, someone objects, how can you present this sonnet as the record of an experience peculiar to Wordsworth? On your own showing, is not this London the summation of English history and spiritual being? Is not his subject analogous to that of Homer in the Iliad; and does he not invite us, like the Greek poet, to rejoice collectively in what there is to yield pride to men of his race? Well, yes, that cannot be denied, and I would not wish to dwell too heavily on what distinguishes one type of poetry from another. Poetry is all one; and the types are more notable for what they have in common than for their differences. That we may all participate in Wordsworth's emotion over what he sees from Westminster Bridge is what makes the poem good as a social exercise. Whatever is purely personal may have high value for the composer, but there would be no point in giving it the dignity of print. One measure of a poem's excellence is the number of readers whose own experience finds expression in it and the fullness and variousness of the expression it finds.

And yet it is clear that this poem was written to record

A ROMANTIC VIEW OF POETRY

the feelings of William Wordsworth on a particular occasion and is an item in his private history. He was personally present and took in with his own eyes the vision of beauty here set down. And he refers in the poem to the reaction which he underwent as an individual in its presence.

But the poem is lyrical in a much deeper sense than that. This city of London, which reminds him of the historical nobility of Englishmen and the spiritual unity of man, reminds him also, though he says nothing of this, of the years he spent there in early manhood, in sorrow and remorse, in poverty and disesteem, with mind and heart divided, meditating how to make a career, and working out a philosophy of life. That at least is the picture of him generally given by his biographers in the years which he has left so obscure. Annette and his child were left in France while the wars went on; and there are many evidences of how deeply he was affected by a situation to which he never refers. He is thought at this period to have been a radical in politics, religion, and social theory. And however much the young man may have prided himself on his emancipation from prejudice and tradition, we know that he must have been the field of a long and desperate conflict between these liberal ideas and conservative instincts deeply rooted in him from infancy. His later views were forming in him, and they must be rationalized with an agony of thought which he has recorded in "The Prelude." In 1802 he had come a long way on his path of reformation; his personal affairs had been settled in a fairly satisfactory manner; he was enjoying a moment of calm, of comparative peace of mind. But the London he viewed from the bridge that July morning * must have been impregnated with associations powerfully

* In Wordsworth's own editions he mistakenly states that the sonnet was composed September 3, but elsewhere he says it was "written on the roof of a coach, on my way to France," which definitely dates it July 31.

70

moving, more immediately personal to him than English history or the conscience of the race.

On October 4 Wordsworth would be married to Mary Hutchinson. On this morning of July 31 he and his sister were taking the Dover coach — he was on his way to Calais for his famous last meeting with "poor Annette," as Dorothy called her. He was going to make the acquaintance of his daughter Caroline, the "dear Child" whom he addresses in the sonnet, "It was a beauteous evening, calm and free." It is clear enough with what heightened sensibility he must have taken his view of London in the early morning from that Dover coach. Of what we may call his personal feelings at the sight of London Wordsworth says nothing, but we may be sure they were powerfully present to color and support what he has to say about it in its impersonal aspect. And to the tone of his personal feeling we must attribute much of the warmth and emotional sweep that give to this sonnet its mysterious power.

But for those who will have a lyric of still more obviously personal reference, let me propose another from Wordsworth. It is one of a group of poems inspired by his famous Scottish walking tour, three of them suggested by the sight of highland lasses. These highland girls made a vivid impression on Wordsworth's imagination; and he makes what in another poet would be an admission that he was sentimentally attracted to one of them. He imagines the pleasure of dwelling with her in some heathy dell as shepherd and shepherdess ("Come live with me and be my Love, And we will all the pleasures prove . . . "). She was really no more to him than a lovely feature of the landscape, but he would like to be kin to her in some way.

> Thou art to me but as a wave
> Of the wild sea: and I would have
> Some claim upon thee, if I could,

> Though but of common neighbourhood.
> What joy to hear thee, and to see!
> Thy elder Brother I would be,
> Thy Father — anything to thee!

Now, do not mistake me. I am not remotely suggesting that there was anything improper in Wordsworth's feelings toward this young girl, any trace of conscious eroticism in his attitude, or disloyalty to his wife at Dove Cottage. But Wordsworth was a poet and a man, and he had, I assume, an unexpended store of that susceptibility to feminine charm which is no respecter of age or social condition. His sister Dorothy was his companion on this tour, and she has recorded the meeting with the highland girl with as much interest as her brother, but with no hint of the personal note that he sounds, and with this other significant difference that, instead of one, it was two girls they met. However, William Wordsworth was not a man to follow the casual promptings of erotic imagination. And a circumstance out of which Shelley would have developed an "Epipsychidion" and Byron a "Maid of Athens" and an *affaire du coeur* was used by Wordsworth merely to add the human note to a set of associations forever dear to him on grounds other than those supplied by Eros.

In the first of these poems the highland girl is made to symbolize that innocence and spontaneity of feeling and manner which he always connected with residence in wild and beautiful places. The place of meeting was on Loch Lomond, and a waterfall, a little bay, and a secluded ferry-house make up the constellation of picturesque items which, together with the girl, impressed him so deeply that in his seventy-third year he still had the most vivid remembrance of them.

> For I, methinks, till I grow old,
> As fair before me shall behold,

As I do now, the cabin small,
The lake, the bay, the waterfall;
And Thee, the Spirit of them all!

This conclusion brings the poem in line with many others in which Wordsworth dwells lovingly on the long continuance in his mind of certain impressions of beauty. In their modest way, they remind one of his doctrine, developed in "The Prelude," of particular "spots of time" which sink so deeply into the poet's imagination, being as they are the effect of his creative power, that they continue to operate in his esthetic being through many years, to reinforce one another, and to build up to something substantial and of peculiar value in his spiritual life. Another of these more modest impressions is that recorded in the famous poem about the daffodils which, as time goes on, continue to

flash upon that inward eye
Which is the bliss of solitude.

And still another is found in the third one of the poems on highland lasses, "The Solitary Reaper," in which Wordsworth describes the girl cutting grain in a mountain valley and singing a song in Gaelic. He longs to know the subject of her song — whether of "old, unhappy, far-off things, and battles long ago," or some more humble lay,

Some natural sorrow, loss, or pain,
That has been, and may be again.

And then he adds, in conclusion,

Whate'er the theme, the Maiden sang
As if her song could have no ending;
I saw her singing at her work,
And o'er the sickle bending; —
I listened — motionless and still;
And when I mounted up the hill,
The music in my heart I bore,
Long after it was heard no more.

In "Stepping Westward," which I will give entire, there is also some suggestion of this lingering reverberation of beauty in the mind. The main theme of the poem is connected with Wordsworth's favorite recreation, walking.

> "*What, you are stepping westward?*" — "*Yea.*"
> — 'Twould be a *wildish* destiny,
> If we, who thus together roam
> In a strange Land, and far from home,
> Were in this place the guests of Chance:
> Yet who would stop, or fear to advance,
> Though home or shelter he had none,
> With such a Sky to lead him on?
>
> The dewy ground was dark and cold;
> Behind, all gloomy to behold;
> And stepping westward seemed to be
> A kind of *heavenly* destiny:
> I liked the greeting; 'twas a sound
> Of something without place or bound;
> And seemed to give me spiritual right
> To travel through that region bright.
>
> The voice was soft, and she who spake
> Was walking by her native Lake:
> The salutation had to me
> The very sound of courtesy:
> Its power was felt; and while my eye
> Was fixed upon the glowing Sky,
> The echo of the voice enwrought
> A human sweetness with the thought
> Of travelling through the world that lay
> Before me in my endless way.

Well, to be sure, this is something more than ordinary pedestrianism. "Travelling through the world" is a phrase around which cluster thick, for anyone, emotional associations of many sorts; in this case is involved the element of adventure and hazard, the possibility of finding oneself without home or shelter. Travelling into the light is another thought that is moving for anyone, even when it is not connected with the thought of going west. For Wordsworth, it was a kind of heavenly destiny; and at this period of his life the word "heavenly" would carry some lurking reminder to him of his heavenly home beyond the grave. But not counting that possible religious association, we may be sure that destiny and westward travel were both connected in his mind with the great psychological principle of hope. For, as he says in "The Prelude,"

> Whether we be young or old,
> Our destiny, our being's heart and home,
> Is with infinitude, and only there;
> With hope it is, hope that can never die,
> Effort, and expectation, and desire,
> And something evermore about to be.

And then, if we add the strain of "human sweetness" which, through a woman's courtesy, was enwrought with the other satisfactions of stepping westward, we realize what a crowded cluster of permanent delight poetic contemplation can conjure out of the homeliest circumstances. It is a part of Wordsworth's private life, but it is something that anyone can enjoy by reference to his own experience.

Anyone, that is, whose taste is prepared to relish imaginative appeals so quiet and unobtrusive. This is not one of the most obviously enchanting of Wordsworth's poems, and Wordsworth is not one of the most obviously enchanting of poets. His effects are most often like "violets by a mossy stone, half hidden from the eye." You have to win a certain intimacy with him before you begin to appreciate all that lies delicately implied in many of his quietest passages. You have indeed to love him before you can begin to do him justice. He says himself of the poet in general:

> He is retired as noontide dew,
> Or fountain in a noonday grove;

And you must love him, ere to you
He will seem worthy of your love.

* * *

And now let us turn to other poets to discover other and
stranger ways in which the poetic alchemy is wrought. Let
us begin with Shelley, and with a poem of universally acknowledged beauty and power, which will be a sharp challenge to our theories. I will give it entire, so that this lovely
thing may not suffer from amputations at our hands.

Lines

When the lamp is shattered,
The light in the dust lies dead;
When the cloud is scattered,
The rainbow's glory is shed;
When the lute is broken,
Sweet tones are remembered not;
When the lips have spoken,
Loved accents are soon forgot.

As music and splendour
Survive not the lamp and the lute,
The heart's echoes render
No song when the spirit is mute: —
No song but sad dirges,
Like the wind through a ruined cell,
Or the mournful surges
That ring the dead seaman's knell.

When hearts have once mingled,
Love first leaves the well-built nest;
The weak one is singled
To endure what it once possesst.
O Love! who bewailest
The frailty of all things here,
Why choose you the frailest
For your cradle, your home, and your bier?

> Its passions will rock thee,
> As the storms rock the ravens on high:
> Bright reason will mock thee,
> Like the sun from a wintry sky.
> From thy nest every rafter
> Will rot, and thine eagle home
> Leave thee naked to laughter
> When leaves fall and cold winds come.

Shelley here makes use of generalizations of the widest reference and comparisons of classic simplicity and familiar power — lamp, rainbow, broken lute, and bird's nest. There is nowhere in the poem anything mawkishly personal in tone. Yet I have the authority of no one less than Professor Newman White that in this poem Shelley is thinking explicitly of himself, and that it is himself he refers to as the frailest one chosen by Love for his cradle, his home, and his bier. And the problem that most insistently confronts us is how to square this lyrical record of grief and disenchantment with my simple notion of poetry as enabling us to realize the satisfaction that we take in living. How can it be, as Shelley asserts elsewhere, that "our sweetest songs are those that tell of saddest thought"?

My answer is a very simple one, as simple as the theory itself. Grief and disenchantment are by no means satisfactions in themselves. Far be it from me to assert anything so unreasonable. It would be like saying, with Pope, "whatever is, is right," and much more childish than that, for I suspect that, in its context, Pope's saying makes a good deal of sense. Grief and disenchantment are in themselves unmitigated evils, and nothing can do away with them or lead us to paint in bright colors the dreary shadow they cast over human existence. But the expression of grief and disenchantment in poetic form may yield satisfactions of the highest order.

77

To begin with, the making of a poem is an art like any other; and artistic creation is one of the leading satisfactions available to men. That is something we have not yet considered. It is a fresh aspect of our subject, and something that must be taken into account in our discussion of the multiple functioning of poetry. When I speak of the arts, I have in mind not merely the so-called fine arts, but all activities in which materials of any sort are manipulated and given shape. It matters not how utilitarian is the object, the esthetic element enters in wherever one is concerned with neatness, finish, rightness, suiting of the means to the end. The carpenter certainly takes an esthetic satisfaction in so hanging a door that it fits well into jamb and lintel and leaves no place for rain and wind to penetrate. The antique dealer shows with pride a highboy which has come down for two hundred years, and the drawers still true. Perhaps no form of satisfaction is more universal than that which men take in the work of their hands. Most business and professional men have their hobbies, their workbench in the basement; some even have their private railroad train in the attic, with all the cars of their own building. The professor of medicine spends the month of January fashioning flies for his August fishing. I know a Czech butcher in a poor quarter who has two main sources of pride — one is the invariable excellence of his cuts of meat; the other is the giant dahlias he raises in his suburban yard. In September you will find them ranged in great vases in his butcher shop. Some of the flowers are a foot broad, but these, he assures me, are not the prettiest. He is as much concerned with variety and loveliness of form as he is with prize-winning bigness; and most of all perhaps with conditions of soil and planting and fertilizing most favorable to the nurture of dahlias. In his delight in dahlias two powerful sentiments collaborate — pride and the love of beauty — and in the love of beauty we can distinguish the love for the beautiful thing and pleasure taken in bringing it to birth.

We need not follow this satisfaction up the scale to the fine arts. We are accustomed to think of the pleasure taken by the composer in adapting some traditional and complicated form to the exigencies of his new theme and tonal system. I have a young friend whom the army has snatched from his promising career as a painter. He has fortunately fallen among officers of discrimination, ready to take into account the training and aptitudes of their conscripts, and has been commissioned to paint a large screen for the officers' mess. His subject is nothing less than a fox hunt. His letters are full of the technical problems involved in this undertaking, which has reconciled him to the life of a private. The screen consists of several panels, of such and such dimensions, and the figures will have to be one third life-size. Men, horses, fox, costume will all have to be studied, and the incidents of a fox hunt adjusted to the size and number of the panels. Then there will be the question of proper medium and ground, the arrangement of colors and forms, and the general problem of style and spirit. Army life is hardly the choice of a young artist just launched in his career, and with a recent bride left behind him. But if there can be any set of conditions to balance these evils, it is such as I have described, in which some scope is given for the exercise of one's chosen craft.

When it comes to poetic art, we know that no poem is written without the facing of many enchanting problems, involving the adjustment of subject and sentiment to genre, metrical form, and traditional style. The very management of the rhymes is an agreeable challenge to the poet, as anyone knows who has ever undertaken a sonnet or a ballad. In the face of all these difficulties it is a great delight to the poet to see his work growing and thriving and establishing itself; a pleasure shared in some measure by any reader who has the least notion of the factors involved.

Now, suppose the subject of the poem is the sufferings of the poet. Then there are two main facts that stand side by side in the poet's consciousness. One is his sufferings and the other is his poetic creation. And one hardly knows which to regard as the more important. We do not need to ignore the poet's sufferings in order to give due weight to the satisfaction taken in his poetic activity. The song of Shelley's which we are considering was written in 1822, the year of his death. For several years he had suffered keenly from depression of mind, caused in part by his disappointment with the course of public affairs. Some of the poems of this period, like "Hellas," reflect the decline of his hopes for improvement in the general condition of men. The exultant note of the lyric, "The world's great age begins anew," and the desperate platonism of his view of death in "Adonais," are hardly more than efforts to throw off the prevailingly gloomy view of man's estate, and the lyric that begins so exultantly concludes with a despondent note:

> Oh, cease! must hate and death return?
>   Cease! must men kill and die?
> Cease! drain not to its dregs the urn
>   Of bitter prophecy.
> The world is weary of the past,
> Oh, might it die or rest at last!

In the song, "When the lamp is shattered," it is the poet's private disillusionment which is the theme — the fatal decay of the sentiment of love, leaving the erstwhile lover to "endure what he once possesst." The most original and moving note in his treatment of this subject is his emphasis on the rational judgment which the mind passes on the frailties of the heart. It is not merely that love withers away or that the passions of love are stormy and leave one homeless. The worst of it all is that one's sentimental nature becomes the object of scorn to oneself and the world.

> Its passions will rock thee,
> As the storms rock the ravens on high:
> Bright reason will mock thee,
> Like the sun from a wintry sky.
> From thy nest every rafter
> Will rot, and thine eagle home
> Leave thee naked to laughter,
> When leaves fall and cold winds come.

The most poignant touch in the whole poem is in the lines,

> Bright reason will mock thee
> Like the sun from a wintry sky.

No critic could possibly pass a severer judgment on Shelley's romanticism than he there passes himself in a moment of despondency. Reason is like the cold white light of the sun in winter falling upon his warm, breathing world of sentiment and freezing it with its mockery.

There is no mitigation of the mood in Shelley's song; and the darkness of his spirit remains unrelieved. And yet this and "Adonais" and the lyric from "Hellas" we class among his finest performances. They are, to use Whitman's feeling phrase, "retrievements out of the night." They are so much forced from the reluctant hands of fate. During the years of his depression, the writing of poetry remained for Shelley an occupation, a solace, and a positive source of delight.

Thus far we have considered lyric poetry dealing with the author's distress in the light of a compensation, something to balance the distress itself. But that takes us only a certain way into the subject. Much of the rationale of this sort of art lies deeper, and there are several steps yet to be taken in the discovery of it. Our first step is the simple recognition that a theme involving sadness and evil may be among the best of themes for literary art.

To have made a thing of beauty out of one's own distress is, to begin with, a greater triumph over circumstance than to have made it out of something pleasing and lovely in itself. To turn the tragedy of life into something sublime is to put the dragon under one's foot, like Saint Michael, and tower above evil in the majesty of one's intellectual being.

And this is true even though the evil is grounded in a weakness of the writer's own character. The English race is generally reputed to be most ridden with the irrational vice of snobbishness — by which I mean the disposition to gauge one's own and others' worth by the superficial standard of social importance. I don't know whether it is true that the English are the greatest snobs; they certainly have their share of this vice. What is more obvious is that, in their prose fiction, they have given the most convincing and most amusing representation of this disposition of mind. They seem to understand it best and have done the most to make it ridiculous. So far as I know there is nothing in French or Russian fiction to compare in this respect with the work of Dickens, Trollope, Thackeray, and Meredith.

In the case of Meredith this constant and conscious satirizing of snobbishness is carried out in spite of the fact that he was himself deeply tainted with the vice. As a mature man he was so ashamed of the fact that he was the son of a tailor that he would never even name the place of his birth. And yet in *Evan Harrington* he has dramatized very much his own situation; he has made ridiculous the sisters of Evan, all of whose efforts were to escape from the stigma of inferior birth, and who went to the greatest pains to keep the family skeleton hidden; and he has given his hero the credit of throwing off this weakness in the end.

Nor is this the only case in which Meredith made his

personal weakness the subject of his comic treatment. Toward his first wife Meredith showed himself wanting in magnanimity. Not only would he not take her back after her brief elopement with another man; for a time he would not let her see their son; and even on her deathbed he would not go to see her. In *The Ordeal of Richard Feverel*, Sir Austin is shown to be equally unforgiving toward his erring wife. We are made to feel that, in his case, it was not so much his love which had been hurt as his pride, his self-esteem, and this is noted as a sign of sentimental egoism in many of Meredith's male characters. One cannot but think it much to an author's credit to be able to give so understanding a representation of his own peculiar weaknesses.

Of course, one might say that, from a moral point of view, getting rid of his vices would be even better than taking them for a subject of artistic representation. And we should all agree. In Meredith's case, indeed, I am inclined to think that he made in the course of his life considerable progress in subduing his meaner propensities. But subduing one's vices is a very difficult business. Just acknowledging them is something, even from the moral point of view. From the intellectual point of view it is a genuine accomplishment. And from the point of view of esthetics it is a notable triumph to have them represented in an effective work of art.

But taking the thing more largely, and without regard to the author's own case, it should be noted that evil and ugliness are among the most promising of subjects for artistic treatment. This is a truth so universally assumed by the great critics of literature that it would not be worth mentioning here except that it is so largely ignored by persons who pretend to a critical approach. This is especially true of one's acquaintances in the business and professional worlds who are wide readers and, generally speaking, persons of cultivated tastes, but who, in their comments on books and pictures and music, are constantly complaining about what they call unpleasant subjects.

In the matter of fiction, I have observed that in general people do not like to meet with a satirical or merely realistic representation of situations and types which too nearly resemble what they are familiar with in their own class or group, and above all in themselves. Thus many Boston readers cannot stomach the novels of Marquand, and even readers outside of Boston are made uneasy by his exposure of something in their own way of thought. The main theme of Marquand in *The Late George Apley* and *H. M. Pulham, Esquire* is the dry rot that comes into the living of people who mistake one narrow set of social values for the primary values in living. But this confusion is so widespread among people of secure position, and the clearing up of this state of mind would result in so much inconvenience and readjustment in their way of life and thought, that the mere representation of their case in fiction takes on the aspect of a major threat to their complacency.

Similar resistances are put up by other groups to other topics that offend them in a similar way. And the poor are no more exempt than the rich. Most people resort to reading from motives that are by no means purely esthetic, unless we take that word in a very broad sense. They go to fiction mainly for what we may call sentimental self-indulgence, and they expect to be flattered and beguiled. They have, no doubt, a genuine psychological need for such beguilement and flattery, and I don't think we should object to their taking such ways as are available for securing them. But this particular sentimental need of readers to protect their own egos should not be made the occasion for ruling out, as improper, themes that to other and tougher minds are among the strongest in esthetic appeal. It should not be made the excuse for condemning in our own times subjects and styles which the best critics have been eager to praise in Greek or Elizabethan literature. And professional students of literary history should be the last to fall into this confusion of "unpleasant" subject matter with inartistic work.

Yet I find that this disposition is not much less general among teachers of literature than among doctors and brokers and truck drivers. Men whose specialty is Jonathan Swift or Alexander Pope are almost as prone to complain, of a new book, that it is too painful or its subject matter too unpleasant; and those whose specialty is Wycherley and Vanbrugh, that is too low. I have no doubt that in many cases there are good esthetic reasons for giving the new book a poor rating; that the low or painful subject has not been so handled as to bring out its true artistic values. But the professor does not always go into the matter with so much discrimination. Too often his comment leaves the impression that the book is to be condemned simply on its subject matter.

Now, this is by no means a simple question, and I do not feel certain that I can trace the causes of this critical confusion. It seems possible, however, that they are somehow related to the confusions that hover round the word "beauty" as it is applied in the fine arts. The word "beauty" is far from easy to define, and it has been taken in many senses. But it is perhaps most frequently used as meaning whatever is pleasing to the eye of the average man, like bright and warm color and ideal proportions in a woman's face and figure. In literature, which deals with human nature, this is extended to cover character and sentiments and ways of living that are pleasing to meet with in actual experience. But if beauty is confined to this meaning, and beauty demanded as a *sine qua non* of good writing, it would simply rule out a large part of what has been approved as literature of the highest class. If you will consider how hard it is to find ideal characters either in fiction or drama — not merely a preponderance of ideal characters, but simply individual characters in novel or play which measure up to the ideal standard — you will understand that beauty in this sense will not do as a criterion of excellence in these forms of art.

Croce has made a brave effort to get round this difficulty by defining beauty in a quite different sense; and his theory is among the most arresting monuments of critical thought. He locates beauty neither in the subject nor in the work of art, but in the process by which the subject is expressed or realized in the work of art. His theory brings to the fore what is a most important and much neglected truth in esthetic criticism, most neglected perhaps in literary criticism — namely, that we must take into account as of prime importance in any art the success, the completeness, with which the artist realizes his concept in his work. But I am inclined to think that Croce has stretched too far the meaning of the word "beauty"; indeed, that in thus appropriating it for the artistic process he has left us without a word for something that cannot well do without one. In the following chapter I shall try to explain how I would meet the problem presented by this ambiguous word "beauty."

Poetry as Release of Emotion

"A TIMELY UTTERANCE GAVE THAT THOUGHT RELIEF"

W ITH regard to beauty, I will be as brief as possible. To begin with, as applied to the fine arts we cannot accept the popular notion of beauty as comprising simply what is pleasing to the senses or sentiments of the average man. You have only to talk with artists to realize how different is their approach to a subject from that of the untutored layman.

Suppose it is a painter considering subjects for landscape or portrait. The layman is always bringing to his attention persons or scenes that would make good subjects — the pretty blonde, the mountain panorama, the rosy sunset. "How perfectly lovely!" says the layman. "You should put that in a picture." But as for the painter . . . it is not a subject that interests him for artistic representation. It says nothing to him as an artist. It lacks variety, it lacks character; it would not compose well; it is not his style. The least he can say is that it does not fall within the limits of his selection. The best artists of all time have wanted something more and something less than the layman's notion of beauty.

The idea of esthetic appeal must be present in our conception of the word; and this without doubt involves such factors as balance of elements, proportion, symmetry, unity of effect. These things make their appeal to us, I presume, because of something in our physiological make-up that has determined our whole esthetic psychology. They are certainly called for in a work of art. But a consideration of the approved masterpieces in any art is sufficient to show that these are considerations of the utmost subtlety and complexity and quite beyond the competence of the average man. There may even be certain fundamental criteria more specific, such as the golden section of the Renaissance painters, to which any artist must conform if he would be sure of producing an effect of beauty. But he would be a bold critic in our day who thought he could lay down the law in this matter. The three dramatic unities long passed for such a criterion in literary art; but while many fine plays were produced upon that formula, it has long since been discredited as an absolute prescription for beauty in a play. The example of Shakespeare never confirmed it, and the authority of Aristotle in favor of it was found to be an error of modern critics.

Our notions of beauty are to a considerable degree conventional, varying from race to race, from period to period, and from culture group to culture group. Underlying them all there are, to be sure, certain basic principles grounded in our animal make-up. Many helpful suggestions can be had by the beginning artist from competent practitioners in his field, and much can be learned from the classical masters. But as for the fundamental laws of beauty, nothing like a proper science exists. It is a subject for psychological study, as I conceive it, and such a study has hardly been started.

I am sorry to leave the subject of beauty so much up in the air. But even if I thought I knew the answers, it would take volumes to recite them. In any case they are not essential to our present purpose, and I wish to pass on to other requirements of a work of art which are, for our purpose, more in need of emphasis.

There are other things than beauty which attract an artist to a subject. These may be involved with beauty, but they can be separately named. One of them is character.

Many eminent artists have been as much concerned with what is *characteristic* in nature as with the beautiful. Such are Velasquez and Rembrandt. In Rembrandt you see it in the type of face he chooses for his portraits — his fondness for aged, wrinkled, meditative types. You see it likewise in his concern with chiaroscuro, which goes far beyond the requirements of mere beauty. In later times we might mention the impressionists as a group — Manet, Degas, Renoir — and such offshoots of impressionism as Cézanne. And in Cézanne's case we have merely to mention his great concern with scenery in which he can exploit the underlying stratification, where it is not beauty in the conventional sense that attracts him, or not that alone, but certain characteristics of matter, expressive of various qualities — solidity, angularity — as well as of the forces of nature that work upon it. Energy is another feature of nature that interests painters, as we see it in the Chinese representation of waves. And artists of all types are interested in forces and their balance almost as much as in more conventional effects of beauty.

With literature comes in the interest in human nature; and here again it is clear how intensely the artist is concerned with the characteristic, as well as the energetic or dynamic, in his subject matter. Burns was as much interested in his Jolly Beggars (a sorry lot of vagabonds) as in his pious cotters. Chaucer was as much interested in pardoner and summoner as in knight and squire. Shakespeare was as much interested in Malvolio and Sir Toby as in Viola and Sebastian; as much in Shylock as in Antonio. He took almost as much interest in Iago as in Othello, and at least as much in Lear as in Cordelia. And Othello was made more interesting by his jealousy, though less perfect, than he would have been without it. Lear's folly was but the beginning of his tragedy; but it was necessary in order to give interest to his tragedy, as well as to make it plausible and endurable.

The more one reflects upon it, the more one comes to realize that some element of evil, of ugliness or pain, is essential to most types of literary art. Evil is something to react against; it contributes tension and dynamism to the drama. It gives relief and pattern to the picture of human life. I will not here go into the esthetic motivations suggested by the word "realism." The urge to tell the truth about human nature and life is of course strongly present in poetry. It is perhaps as primary as any other emotional urge, and it yields its own high satisfactions. And simple truthtelling is, I believe, one of the many functions of poetic art that should be taken into account in any complete survey of the subject. But I can only refer to this in passing as one of the motives of the poet in his choice of themes involving elements of ugliness and pain.

What I have said upon this subject is by no means original or novel, but it is so constantly ignored in popular criticism, and popular criticism so largely fills the horizon, that it is necessary to repeat these elementary truths in considering the case of the lyric poet who takes for his theme his own sufferings or the sadness of life in general. But I have by no means come to the end of that subject. I have mentioned the fact that, in singing his own sorrows, the poet is compensating for them in some measure by the delight he takes in the exercise of his art; that he achieves a moral and artistic triumph and in a sense rises above his sorrow in the act of expressing it in terms of poetry. And now I am saying that the lyric poet, aside from the scientific impulse to realism, has as much of an interest as anyone else in choosing a strong subject, and that his own sorrows may well be the strongest subject at his command at the time of writing.

POETRY AS RELEASE OF EMOTION

"At his command," in the sense of well learned, freshly
studied, and deeply impressed on his imagination, which is
the starting point of all poetic activity. Considering the poet
as an artist, we might say that his sorrows are accidental
and his art essential. His sorrows are stuff for his art, and
he may even treat them as objectively and calculatingly as
if they were something quite outside himself. Thus Keats
with his melancholy. We know from his letters that early
in the year 1819 he was suffering from mental depression.
Yet, as he writes to Haydon, "I do not think I shall ever
come to the rope or the pistol, for after a day or two's melancholy, although I smoke more and more of my own insufficiency—I see by little and little more of what is to be
done, and how it is to be done, should I ever be able to do
it. On my soul, there should be some reward for that con-
tinual *agonie ennuyeuse*." In such a state of mind, it is clear
that the melancholy will never wholly gain the ascendancy;
instead, it is obviously destined to become the subject of the
poet's art. And we have that coolly objective and gor-
geously beautiful "Ode on Melancholy."

The first thing that Keats does, by a kind of dramatic
instinct, is to get rid of the first person singular and project
himself dramatically as a person to be addressed in the second person. He is someone of a romantic turn desiring to
taste the pensive delights of melancholy. But he has considered this subject in the abstract, and he knows that for a
true appreciation of all that melancholy has to yield to the
connoisseur, she ought not to be worshipped in the conventional manner, with symbols traditionally associated with
darkness and grief.

> No, no! go not to Lethe, neither twist
>   Wolf's-bane, tight-rooted, for its poisonous wine;
> Nor suffer thy pale forehead to be kiss'd
>   By nightshade, ruby grape of Proserpine;

Make not your rosary of yew-berries,
    Nor let the beetle, nor the death-moth be
        Your mournful Psyche, nor the downy owl
A partner in your sorrow's mysteries;
    For shade to shade will come too drowsily,
        And drown the wakeful anguish of the soul.

Keats's imagination is here proceeding much as Donne's
might. He begins with a paradox and supports that with another. The initial paradox is the assumption that one might
deliberately seek to induce a mood that is painful. The supporting paradox is that developed in this first stanza — that
while melancholy is a dark and shady state, a goddess of
night, she is not best invoked by thoughts of death or of
death's sister, sleep. Lethe is the river of oblivion, in which
death and sleep are associated together. Death is suggested
by poisonous nightshade; by yew berries, signifying ceme-
teries; beetle, ancient symbol of death; and death-moth,
given a wide range of associations by being designated as a
"mournful Psyche." Sleep again is suggested by the "downy
owl," and both sleep and death in that superb, far-fetched
epithet for nightshade, the "ruby grape of Proserpine."
Throughout this and the final stanza of the ode, Keats con-
sistently pursues the figure of melancholy as a goddess, with
her religious cult. The downy owl is not to be made "a
partner in your sorrow's mysteries." You are not to make
your rosary of yew berries. Your pale forehead — pale as
that of a worshipper at a shrine — is not to be wreathed with
nightshade as the temples of the Dionysiac are wreathed
with ivy, or perchance with "vine leaves." Nightshade has
red berries suggestive of "ruby grapes," and, since it is poisonous, it may well be called the grape of Proserpine, queen
of the realm of gloomy Dis. None of these symbols will
serve.

    For shade to shade will come too drowsily,
        And drown the wakeful anguish of the soul.

Melancholy may be a deathly mood, but it is not a sleepy one. It is a "wakeful anguish," an *agonie ennuyeuse*, and it requires the participation of the faculty of enjoyment as well as of sensibility to pain. It is best induced by images of beauty.

> But when the melancholy fit shall fall
>   Sudden from heaven like a weeping cloud,
> That fosters the droop-headed flowers all,
>   And hides the green hill in an April shroud;
> Then glut thy sorrow on a morning rose,
>   Or on the rainbow of the salt sand-wave,
>   Or on the wealth of globèd peonies;
> Or if thy mistress some rich anger shows,
>   Emprison her soft hand, and let her rave,
>   And feed deep, deep upon her peerless eyes.
> She dwells with Beauty . . .

(Not the mistress — she is but an instance in support of a theory. "She" is melancholy itself, of which beauty and delight are notable provocatives.)

> She dwells with Beauty — Beauty that must die;
>   And Joy, whose hand is ever at his lips
> Bidding adieu; and aching Pleasure nigh,
>   Turning to poison while the bee-mouth sips:
> Ay, in the very temple of Delight
>   Veil'd Melancholy has her sovran shrine,
>   Though seen of none save him whose strenuous tongue
> Can burst Joy's grape against his palate fine;
>   His soul shall taste the sadness of her might,
>   And be among her cloudy trophies hung.

I have compared Keats's imaginative process to that of Donne. But there is a closer and more precise comparison to be made. There was an exact contemporary of Keats, a writer most successful in prose, who shared much of Keats's imaginative quality — his fondness for Elizabethan poetry and quaint archaic forms, his penchant for epithets, involved and far-fetched and allusive, his whimsicality, his love of paradox and wit. Charles Lamb is the one writer of that period who might have written what Keats wrote to Haydon: "I do not think I shall ever come to the rope or the pistol, for after a day or two's melancholy, although I smoke more and more of my insufficiency," and so on. He is the one who would most infallibly relish Keats's characterizing nightshade as "ruby grape of Proserpine," or his view of "Joy, whose hand is ever at his lips bidding adieu," or his fancy that Veil'd Melancholy has her sovran shrine in the very temple of Delight. Lamb, moreover, was the man of his time best able to understand how a serious poem might be conceived in terms of what the seventeenth century called wit. And he would understand that a single mood need not be taken as representative of a poet's whole philosophy of life, even when that mood was grounded in a profound psychological truth.

Lamb's personal life was full of tragedy and emotional deprivation; and the iron had entered too deeply into his soul for him to wish, in his own work, to look directly on human nature as in itself it really is. As a writer of essays he is not the realist that Hazlitt is. His disposition is to keep to the surface of human psychology or to sound the depths only where there are pearls to be found. For the most part he skirts the fringes of evil and pain, making the most of eccentricities in character and of all the minor alleviations of our dark lot. He was, we might well say without disparagement, an escapist. But he was, like Keats, a devotee of old Burton. He knew the fascinations of melancholy. And he doubtless understood that no man has tasted life to the full, has reaped the richest emotional and spiritual satisfactions provided by experience, unless he has been subject in some measure to suffering and sadness. I am not referring to Carlyle's romantic Christianism in his "divine sanctuary of

Sorrow." I am thinking of that appreciation of the range of emotional experience necessary to a full life which is a part of any enlightened hedonism.

Lamb, then, would understand how a poet might take for his subject the cult of melancholy, and he would appreciate the proportion of seriousness to paradox in Keats's treatment of it. He would not suppose that, because Keats recommended that the best results could be had by the agency of beauty and joy, or even because he implied that melancholy had its own genuine satisfactions, he had thereby pledged himself irrevocably to a morbid indulgence in melancholy. He would appreciate the spice of wit that informs the whole work as well as the individual strokes of witty fancy by which it is made into one firm imaginative texture.

The "Ode on Melancholy" we have considered as an example of a poet's choosing a sad subject because it is a strong one. But we have not yet exhausted this matter of lyric motivation. Indeed, we have not yet touched on what is probably the profoundest, the most universal, and the primary motive for the taking up of sad subjects. Keats's treatment of melancholy is so objective that it seems to suggest merely the deliberate choice of a strong subject for treatment, whether that subject is derived from personal experience or from simple observation. The profoundest of lyrical motives appears only where it is obvious that the poet is expressing a strong feeling of his own. The primary motive for lyrical poetry is to relieve the feelings, whatever they are. This is what Wordsworth has in mind when he says that "poetry is the spontaneous overflow of powerful feelings." As applied to sad feeling, Wordsworth illustrates this view of poetry in his Intimations ode.

> To me alone there came a thought of grief:
> A timely utterance gave that thought relief,
> And I again am strong.

When an emotion is painful, we speak more naturally of giving it relief. But the process is essentially the same whatever the nature of the emotion. Only, with emotions that are not painful we should use some other word, like "release" or "discharge." We say of joy that it is too great to be contained. It is highly probable that most poetry, when it is the result of a genuine native urge, is in large measure motivated by the need to release or discharge emotions that have accumulated within us to such a degree that to contain them would be distressing. A physiologist would be able to name many analogous cases of release or discharge within our bodily system beneath or above the level of consciousness, and would regard these instinctive or automatic processes as necessary to bodily health. I am confident that a psychologist would take the same view of the need to relieve what we may call congestion in that part of our emotional nature which comes within the range of consciousness.

Act, gesture, word are the means of releasing emotion; and we have an enormous advantage over the lower animal kind in that to the act and gesture which we have in common with them we have added the word. Where behavior is largely instinctive and automatic there is no need for words. But where it is to some extent considered, words become more and more important as a means of expressing emotion. And especially so since considered action implies a very large measure of inhibition upon behavior that is dangerous to ourselves or socially inadmissible. Where action cannot follow on impulse, we have a thousand times more need for the verbal release of emotion. A very great deal of poetry is, in this sense, a sublimation of emotions which it is not allowable or not convenient to express in action.

If this view of poetry as a means of discharging emotion

is thought to bear some resemblance to Aristotle's theory of catharsis in music and tragedy, I should of course be gratified. If I do not claim any such illustrious kinship, it is because I am not a good enough scholar to feel at all confident of my ground when it comes to the interpretation of the Greeks. At any rate, I am pleased to consider that my view, like that of the Stagirite, is essentially psychological in its approach.

It will be objected that I lay too much stress on emotion and too little on the intellectual element, which should predominate in poetry if it is to be first-rate, or even respectable. But here two things are to be noted. I am not considering what poetry *should* be according to some moral or critical standard, but what I believe it to be in essence and in the actual practice of approved poets of all times. And then, with regard to the ratio of emotion to intellect in good poetry I have not expressed an opinion. I have merely said that the primary motivation of much good poetry, perhaps of all good poetry, is emotional; the impulse is emotional. And that is nothing more than I would say of our life in general. The stuff of living is emotion. The intellect comes in to identify the emotion and make us conscious of it, to classify it and bring it into relation with other emotions, to order and systematize our set of emotions, to refine upon them — in short, to shape them. The moment we have found a word, emotion is stamped with intellect; and the simplest verbal expression of emotion is so deeply tinged with thought that we are inclined to mistake it for an intellectual process. It is hard to determine how far emotion is servant of our thought and how far thought is servant of emotion. But we must not forget that the very motivation of our thinking is affective, and that most of our thoughts may be regarded as the generalization or precipitate of earlier feelings.

I have no doubt that there is a hierarchy among poets; that some are superior to others by virtue of the quality of the emotions they express, the degree to which these emotions are made subject to the shaping and ordering power of thought. But what I am here contending is that on any level poetry is largely of service to men as a means of discharging emotions which, if left unexpressed, would remain to poison the system. And of course I have in mind that the reader, in so far as he enters imaginatively into the poet's process, is to some extent participating in this same emotional satisfaction; nay, that in most cases he does so enter into the poet's process because he is subject to the same emotions and in need of a similar discharge, if only vicariously.

In an earlier chapter I have spoken of Byron's "Childe Harold," and how in that poem, when deeply discontented with himself and his personal life, he found a compensatory satisfaction, a new and better life, in recreating what was most inspiring in the history of the lands he visited, *replacing* what was hateful in his own experience with a form of living more desirable. But that is only one of the several strains that go to make up the complicated pattern of these later cantos of "Childe Harold." Byron has not forgotten himself, his loneliness and pride, his separation from those he loves, and above all that twist in his character from which he suffers, to which somehow he must reconcile himself, and which he must make less despicable in the eyes of the world. He is trying to recognize his own weaknesses and to steel himself with a sort of stoic discipline to accept his lot without repining.

> Yet must I think less wildly; — I *have* thought
> Too long and darkly, till my brain became,
> In its own eddy boiling and o'erwrought,
> A whirling gulf of phantasy and flame:
> And thus, untaught in youth my heart to tame,

> My springs of life were poison'd. 'Tis too late!
> Yet am I changed; though still enough the same
> In strength to bear what time cannot abate,
> And feed on bitter fruits without accusing Fate.

He makes several confessions of error and summons himself more than once to stern tasks of self-control in facing good and bad fortune. But most of all what Byron is trying to do in "Childe Harold" is somehow to maintain his self-respect in the face of the world's reprobation. In spite of acknowledged faults he feels that he has been unfairly condemned. With the world so against him, he turns instinctively against the world, made up, as it is, so largely of hypocrites and timeservers, incapable of appreciating such integrity of character as he feels himself to have. He has always been at feud with this world of sycophants.

> I have not loved the world, nor the world me;
> I have not flatter'd its rank breath, nor bow'd
> To its idolatries a patient knee,
> Nor coin'd my cheek to smiles, nor cried aloud
> In worship of an echo; in the crowd
> They could not deem me one of such: I stood
> Among them, but not of them; in a shroud
> Of thoughts which were not their thoughts, and still could,
> Had I not filed my mind, which thus itself subdued.

Then for a moment he pretends to be magnanimous, but his magnanimity yields to as bitterly ironic an estimate of human nature as can be found in English poetry.

> I have not loved the world, nor the world me, —
> But let us part fair foes; I do believe,
> Though I have found them not, that there may be
> Words which are things, hopes which will not deceive,
> And virtues which are merciful nor weave
> Snares for the failing; I would also deem
> O'er others' griefs that some sincerely grieve;
> That two, or one, are almost what they seem,
> That goodness is no name, and happiness no dream.

So it is that his first generous admission that there is virtue
and kindness in the world is whittled away with one sly
attenuation after another until nothing is left but a desperate, sneering hope that goodness is no name and happiness
no dream. It is one of the wittiest performances in nine-
teenth-century verse, and it must have given Byron the
keenest pleasure to pen it.

The stanzas quoted are from the third canto. But it is
in the fourth that Byron compares notes with the world in
the most dramatic and yet most desperately sincere passage.
The Coliseum makes him think of Roman fortitude and of
Nemesis. He grants that through his own fault he is the
proper victim of the Furies; but still he contends that he
has been stabbed in the back by his accusers, and that vengeance is due upon the world that proscribed him. He gives
an ingeniously theatrical turn to this subject of vengeance;
he then recites his wrongs and sufferings in tones of sincerity that cannot be mistaken. And he ends the passage with
his special romantic version of the Horatian "non omnis
moriar."

> It is not that I may not have incurr'd
> For my ancestral faults or mine the wound
> I bleed withal, and, had it been conferr'd
> With a just weapon, it had flow'd unbound;
> But now my blood shall not sink in the ground;
> To thee I do devote it [to Nemesis] — *thou* shalt take
> The vengeance, which shall yet be sought and found,
> Which if I have not taken for the sake —
> But let that pass — I sleep, but thou shalt yet awake.
>
> And if my voice break forth, 'tis not that now
> I shrink from what is suffer'd; let him speak
> Who hath beheld decline upon my brow,
> Or seen my mind's convulsion leave it weak;
> But in this page a record will I seek.
> Not in the air shall these my words disperse,

Though I be ashes; a far hour shall wreak
The deep prophetic fulness of this verse,
And pile on human heads the mountain of my curse!

That curse shall be Forgiveness. Have I not —
Hear me, my mother Earth! behold it, Heaven! —
Have I not had to wrestle with my lot?
Have I not suffer'd things to be forgiven?
Have I not had my brain sear'd, my heart riven,
Hopes sapp'd, name blighted, Life's life lied away?
And only not to desperation driven,
Because not altogether of such clay
As rots into the souls of those whom I survey.

From mighty wrongs to petty perfidy
Have I not seen what human things could do?
From the loud roar of foaming calumny
To the small whisper of the as paltry few,
And subtler venom of the reptile crew,
The Janus glance of whose significant eye,
Learning to lie with silence, would *seem* true,
And without utterance, save the shrug or sigh,
Deal round to happy fools its speechless obloquy.

But I have lived, and have not lived in vain:
My mind may lose its force, my blood its fire,
And my frame perish even in conquering pain;
But there is that within me which shall tire
Torture and Time, and breathe when I expire;
Something unearthly which they deem not of,
Like the remember'd tone of a mute lyre,
Shall on their soften'd spirits sink, and move
In hearts all rocky now the late remorse of love.

I would not put these stanzas forward as poetry of notable distinction, let alone as characterized by that high seriousness that Arnold requires of his classical touchstones. Byron's curse of forgiveness and late remorse of love are a little too stagy for modern taste. As for his way of dealing with a hostile world and his own character, no one could pretend that it is a model of moral wisdom. It is pretty clear that he was a badly spoiled child Harold, with a distinctly pathological strain in his sexual make-up and a morbidly touchy pride, made sore by many a defeat. If, instead of writing "Childe Harold," he could, at the age of twenty-eight, have made himself over into an altruistic, or even a normally social-minded, citizen, it would have been a miracle of grace, and the world would have been the poorer by at least one fine poem. What he did was to follow the usual channels of psychological adjustment. Being a rhetorical genius, he was able to give to his complex emotional state magnificent verbal expression. It was perhaps the only thing that could have saved him from complete collapse. It must have given him a vast deal of satisfaction.

And it was not merely himself for whom it procured such satisfaction. His great popularity with the whole world of European readers was based in something more than the historical episodes — the dying gladiator and the "sound of revelry by night" — or the purple patches of nature worship. In "Childe Harold," as in so many of Byron's earlier and later poems, great numbers of readers responded to the picture of a man on whom the pack has turned — one not without faults, but even so, nobler than the common run who are hounding him, and who have misunderstood and done him grievous wrong — a man who alternately walks alone in silent pride or turns and fights the world when brought to bay. To such a theme men respond, I suppose, because so generally this is the way we feel about ourselves and a mean and unappreciative world. We know how poorly we have done, how defective we are, and yet, to apply Wordsworth's line somewhat differently from what he intended, "we feel that we are greater than we know." We strongly feel that justice has not been done us. And so we find in a poet like Byron some release for emotions which we have not ourselves the boldness nor the skill to express.

As for Byron, it is even a question whether this was not one means by which he managed to find firm footing again in a reeling world. For his behavior appears from that time on to have been greatly normalized. He made some kind of good adjustment in his sentimental life. He settled down to steady, serious work in poetry, and produced such masterpieces as "Manfred," "Don Juan," and "The Vision of Judgment." And at length he found in the cause of Greek independence an exercise of his faculties not unworthy of his moral pretensions and a way to die not unworthy of his Satanic pride. So that perhaps we can suggest with some measure of plausibility that Byron's poetry did actually act "orgiastically" on his soul, so that it "became settled by a kind of medicine and purgation."

It is interesting to note his emotional development between "Childe Harold" and "Don Juan." This has some bearing on the subject referred to, of the ratio between intellect and emotion in poetry. For it shows us a powerful poet making the passage from the lyrical mode to a more objective genre by virtue of the growing prominence of a critical attitude. The clue to this change is found in a flippant passage in the fourth canto of "Don Juan."

> As boy, I thought myself a clever fellow,
>   And wish'd that others held the same opinion;
> They took it up when my days grew more mellow,
>   And other minds acknowledged my dominion:
> Now my sere fancy "falls into the yellow
>   Leaf," and Imagination droops her pinion,
> And the sad truth which hovers o'er my desk
> Turns what was once romantic to burlesque.
>
> And if I laugh at any mortal thing,
>   'Tis that I may not weep; and if I weep,

'Tis that our nature cannot always bring
   Itself to apathy, for we must steep
Our hearts first in the depths of Lethe's spring,
   Ere what we least wish to behold will sleep:
Thetis baptized her mortal son in Styx;
A mortal mother would on Lethe fix.

The great variation in tone which appears even in this brief
passage illustrates the difficulty of precisely defining the
type of poem that Byron is here producing; but the term
"burlesque" will serve well enough to cover the diversity of
elements that enter into it. If he calls it an epic, this is hardly
more than an occasion to assume a tone of humorous complacency in regard to his great undertaking, to pretend to
literary virtues which he obviously does not possess, declare
his allegiance to the English classics, and lay about him at
all his contemporaries; in short, to treat grave subjects with
levity and light subjects with gravity, passing back and
forth continually between the high and the low styles.

My poem's epic, and is meant to be
   Divided in twelve books; each book containing,
With love, and war, a heavy gale at sea,
   A list of ships, and captains, and kings reigning,
New characters; the episodes are three:
   A panoramic view of hell's in training,
After the style of Virgil and of Homer,
So that my name of Epic's no misnomer.

All these things will be specified in time,
   With strict regard to Aristotle's rules,
The *Vade Mecum* of the true sublime,
   Which makes so many poets, and some fools:
Prose poets like blank-verse, I'm fond of rhyme,
   Good workmen never quarrel with their tools;
I've got new mythological machinery,
And very handsome supernatural scenery.

There's only one slight difference between
   Me and my epic brethren gone before.

And here the advantage is my own, I ween
   (Not that I have not several merits more,
But this will more peculiarly be seen);
   They so embellish, that 'tis quite a bore
Their labyrinth of fables to thread through,
Whereas this story's actually true.

If any person doubt it, I appeal
   To history, tradition, and to facts,
To newspapers, whose truth all know and feel,
   To plays in five, and operas in three acts;
All these confirm my statement a good deal,
   But that which more completely faith exacts
Is that myself, and several more in Seville,
Saw Juan's last elopement with the devil.

If ever I should condescend to prose,
   I'll write poetical commandments, which
Shall supersede beyond all doubt all those
   That went before; in these I shall enrich
My text with many things that no one knows,
   And carry precept to the highest pitch:
I'll call the work "Longinus o'er a Bottle,
Or, Every Poet his *own* Aristotle."

Thou shalt believe in Milton, Dryden, Pope;
   Thou shalt not set up Wordsworth, Coleridge, Southey;
Because the first is crazed beyond all hope,
   The second drunk, the third so quaint and mouthy:
With Crabbe it may be difficult to cope,
   And Campbell's Hippocrene is somewhat drouthy:
Thou shalt not steal from Samuel Rogers, nor
Commit — flirtation with the muse of Moore.

Byron's satire — literary, political, and social — is not an
attack in form, but consists in a series of running hits, de-
livered in the burlesque manner, and incidental to his trav-
esty of the epic. He dedicates his poem to that "epic Rene-
gade," Bob Southey, author of many tedious and pretentious
narrative poems. He has it in for Southey because, as laure-

ate of a reactionary government, he is implicated in the public crime of the bloody subjection of Ireland and all Europe. Wordsworth and Coleridge come under the same ban for the same political reasons, as well as for the obscurity and prosiness of their writings.

> And Wordsworth, in a rather long *Excursion*
> (I think the quarto holds five hundred pages),
> Has given a sample from the vasty version
> Of his new system to perplex the sages.

As for Coleridge, who has offered an extensive and dark exposition of his system in *Biographia Literaria* —

> And Coleridge, too, has lately taken wing,
> But like a hawk encumber'd with his hood, —
> Explaining metaphysics to the nation —
> I wish he would explain his Explanation.

In the character of Don Juan's mother, Byron manages to give a very lively malicious portrait of his wife, in which every thrust grows out of an apparent compliment by way of innuendo and burlesque descent from the serious to the trivial.

> Her favourite science was the mathematical,
> Her noblest virtue was her magnanimity,
> Her wit (she sometimes tried at wit) was Attic all,
> Her serious sayings darken'd to sublimity;
> In short, in all things she was fairly what I call
> A prodigy — her morning dress was dimity,
> Her evening silk, or, in the summer, muslin,
> And other stuffs, with which I won't stay puzzling.
> . . . .
> In short, she was a walking calculation,
> Miss Edgeworth's novels stepping from their covers,
> Or Mrs. Trimmer's books on education,
> Or "Coelebs' Wife" set out in quest of lovers,
> Morality's prim personification,
> In which not Envy's self a flaw discovers;

> To others' share let "female errors fall,"
> For she had not even one — the worst of all.

The Don Juan legend, which Byron adapts with the utmost freedom of invention, is hardly more than the starting point for a series of lively adventures, conducted in a rather picaresque manner, which take the hero from Spain to Greece, and thence to Constantinople, to Russia, and finally to England, and enable Byron to make his satirical comment on European political and social life. It amounts in the end to a sort of comprehensive burlesque of contemporary culture and civilization.

In the final cantos, recounting Juan's amours in England, Byron has a chance to give his satirical estimate of the English character as exhibited in what is called "society," "amongst a people famous for reflection, who like to play the fool with circumspection."

This poem is not autobiographical like "Childe Harold," though Byron often takes occasion to speak *in propria persona*. In so far as it is an expression of his own spiritual state, it is a vehicle for making fun of himself as a representative of a romantic race and age. Over and over again, a passage begins in a romantic vein worthy of "Childe Harold" only to pass by swift transition into hard-boiled realism or cynical flippancy. The account of storm and shipwreck in the second canto is a curious mélange of picturesque description, pathos, tragedy, with details commonplace or shocking, as the reporter's mind ranges from the throwing over board of hen coops to the practice of cannibalism under threat of starvation. The one thing Byron reports with least qualified admiration is the love of Juan and Haidée, "Nature's bride," absolutely unaffected by social or bookish convention, and more than once the poet is on the point of growing sentimental over this thoroughly romantic situation, when he pulls himself up sharp. He is describing the walk taken by the lovers along the wild coast of Haidée's island, and is on the point of losing himself in the double piety of love and nature; but he thinks better of it and goes on smoothly:

> And the small ripple spilt upon the beach
>   Scarcely o'erpass'd the cream of your champagne,
> When o'er the brim the sparkling bumpers reach,
>   That spring-dew of the spirit! the heart's rain!
> Few things surpass old wine; and they may preach
>   Who please, — the more because they preach in vain, —
> Let us have wine and women, mirth and laughter,
> Sermons and soda-water the day after.

Even his devotion to the cause of national freedom is not exempt from the burlesque turn; and the famous lyric "The Isles of Greece" is immediately followed by a series of disillusioned reflections on the sincerity of poets.

In his general burlesque survey of human nature, Byron does not forget to include himself. The tone is very different from that of "Childe Harold," though frequently he starts out in such a strain or lapses into it momentarily.

> But now at thirty years my hair is grey
>   (I wonder what it will be like at forty?
> I thought of a peruke the other day) —
>   My heart is not much greener; and, in short, I
> Have squander'd my whole summer while 'twas May,
>   And feel no more the spirit to retort; I
> Have spent my life, both interest and principal,
> And deem not, what I deem'd, my soul invincible.

> No more — no more — Oh! never more on me
>   The freshness of the heart can fall like dew,
> Which out of all the lovely things we see
>   Extracts emotions beautiful and new;
> Hived in our bosoms like the bag o' the bee:
>   Think'st thou the honey with those objects grew?
> Alas! 'twas not in them, but in thy power
> To double even the sweetness of a flower.

No more — no more — Oh! never more, my heart,
   Canst thou be my sole world, my universe!
Once all in all, but now a thing apart,
   Thou canst not be my blessing or my curse:
The illusion's gone for ever, and thou art
   Insensible, I trust, but none the worse,
And in thy stead I've got a deal of judgment,
Though heaven knows how it ever found a lodgment.

My days of love are over; me no more
   The charms of maid, wife, and still less of widow,
Can make the fool of which they made before, —
   In short, I must not lead the life I did do;
The credulous hope of mutual minds is o'er,
   The copious use of claret is forbid too,
So for a good old-gentlemanly vice
I think I must take up with avarice.

Byron says that now, instead of illusions, he has got a
deal of judgment. And certain it is that the critical intellect
is in the ascendant in the conduct of his narrative. Does that
mean that he is no longer a bundle of emotions, or that he
is no longer seeking in poetry the release of his feelings?
By no means. His subject is still his emotional attitudes toward himself and the world. Only, now he will not wear
his heart on his sleeve, or not long enough to give an adversary a stab at it. In his attitude toward himself he summons
wit to the defense of his sensibilities. With a world that has
misjudged him, he still keeps up his feud. But he has assumed the whole armory of burlesque to help him in the
fight, and instead of standing on defense, he has chosen
the stronger tactic of carrying the war into the enemy's
country. "Don Juan" was an electrical storm of the first
magnitude, at which all Europe looked on with delighted
interest. A vast deal of emotional energy was released. And
both for Byron and for Europe it did a lot to clear the air.

Poetry as Dialectic

"THE MANY-MINDED SOUL OF MAN"

ONE may complain that Byron lacks an integrated, or at any rate a constructive, philosophy. No soul could live on the diet he provides without supplementing it from other sources richer in vitamins. In this respect, the difference between what he has to give and the offering of a poet like Shelley is indicated by comparing his poem on Prometheus, written in 1816, with Shelley's "Prometheus Unbound," dating from some two or three years later. Byron sees the Titan still bound, still the victim of his own virtues.

> Thy Godlike crime was to be kind,
>   To render with thy precepts less
>   The sum of human wretchedness,
> And strengthen man with his own mind . . .

Even in bonds Prometheus is of service to man in teaching him to bear his fate with stoical endurance.

> Thou art a symbol and a sign
>   To Mortals of their fate and force;
> Like thee, Man is in part divine,
>   A troubled stream from a pure source;
> And Man in portions can foresee
> His own funereal destiny,
> His wretchedness, and his resistance,
> And his sad unallied existence:
> To which his Spirit may oppose
> Itself — and equal to all woes,
>   And a firm will, and a deep sense,
> Which even in torture can descry
>   Its own concenter'd recompense,
> Triumphant where it dares defy,
> And making Death a Victory.

Thus Byron's Prometheus does not get farther than his Manfred. It is not a strictly stoical position, for his existence is seen as "unallied," whereas the first principle of the stoics was to identify themselves with the great beneficent powers of the universe. Prometheus and Manfred, in their noble but dreary individualism, have only the sour comfort of possessing their own souls. And in their desperate realism, they have only the cold comfort of accepting the tragic truth. The advantage of Shelley's Prometheus, and what makes him a fuller embodiment of the Greek myth than Byron's figure, is that, being a type of humanity taken collectively, he is not shut up in a proud individualism, and, being a type of man's progressive or idealistic disposition, he is not confined to a sterile realism.

The life of the imagination has two poles, the real and the ideal, and poetry is in perpetual oscillation between these poles. One of our strongest and most normal passions is the passion for the truth. Our intellectual nature and our moral nature alike drive us to the finding and the publishing of the truth. It is not merely that truth is essential for so dealing with the facts as to make the best of them. Our very pride as upright and thinking animals forces us to look the facts in the face and shout them from the housetops. The scientific drive is part of our make-up as thinking beings — the powerful urge to understand the facts and trace the laws that operate in each realm of knowledge. And because I hold this to be one of the noblest of our endowments, I cannot join in the criticism so often levelled at the realistic school of fiction, especially at the realists of the great period in France — men like Zola and Flaubert. They do not represent the whole of art; the truth they tell is certainly not the whole story. But so far as it goes, it is the truth — it is the truth as they see it. The passion of science joined in them with the passion of art, and what they wrought was one of the great monuments to the creative impulse.

But there is another pole to the imagination which is just as valid and important as the realistic. Whatever the facts of life, they derive half their meaning for us from our idea of what can be made of them.

> Our destiny, our being's heart and home,
> Is with infinitude, and only there;
> With hope it is, hope that can never die,
> Effort, and expectation, and desire,
> And something evermore about to be.

We believe that men have the faculty of fixing goals and striving for their attainment. We believe that such striving is itself a fact of life — the most important fact of all, since it is the means by which the will of man is made effectual in the world of fact. We believe further that certain goals are more worth while than others, since they represent our most persistent notions of human well-being. Such goals we call *ideals*. They have their origin in our moral sense, our vision of better and worse; and it is by reference to them that we organize our most serious activities. Such an ideal is justice among men — the heart's demand that all men should be treated without discrimination and given their chance for happiness. Another ideal, which comprehends justice, is the ideal of brotherly love. It seems to us good that men should live in relations of mutual affection and well-being; that they should strive together for a common good. We deeply feel that the good of life is multiplied when it is thus shared. This is the moral ideal that underlies the political theory of democracy. I am tired of having cynical people dismiss democracy as a mere device for securing the widest distribution of material goods. I am tired of having them treat the ideal of progress as if that was all it meant. The best of those who have written of progress and democracy have always had in mind as chief gain a growth in brotherly love, in mutuality. They have held that the ends sought were good in large part because they were shared by human beings who feel toward one another like members of the same family.

If, then, men's active lives are directed toward ideal goals, it is inevitable that such ideals should play a large part in their imaginative creation. It is by reference to such ideals that the life of the imagination may be *oriented*, like our life in action. And it is a commonplace of psychology, as it is of literary criticism, that in the long run the life of the imagination is not without its effect on our life in action. One of the most impressive statements of this truth is made by Shelley in his "Defense of Poetry." It is in connection with the frequent charge of immorality brought against the poets. "The whole objection," he says, "of the immorality of poetry

rests upon a misconception of the manner in which poetry acts to produce the moral improvement of man. Ethical science arranges the elements which poetry has created, and propounds schemes and proposes examples of civil and domestic life; nor is it for want of admirable doctrines that men hate, and despise, and censure, and deceive, and subjugate one another. But poetry acts in another and diviner manner. It awakens and enlarges the mind itself by rendering it the receptacle of a thousand unapprehended combinations of thought. Poetry lifts the veil from the hidden beauty of the world, and makes familiar objects be as if they were not familiar; it reproduces all that it represents, and the impersonations clothed in its Elysian light stand thenceforward in the minds of those who have once contemplated them, as memorials of that gentle and exalted content which extends itself over all thoughts and actions with which it coexists. The great secret of morals is love; or a going out of our own nature, and an identification of ourselves with the beautiful which exists in thought, action, or person, not our own.

Now, Shelley's Prometheus and Asia are such "impersonations" clothed in the Elysian light of the poet's thought. In view of his role in the poem and what is said of him, Prometheus is best regarded as a representative of the ideal or progressive aspects of humankind. The backward drag of selfish interest and tradition is represented by Jupiter. The poem has often been misinterpreted by critics, who have taken Jupiter for a god and a principle of evil quite outside human nature; and Shelley's conception of evil has been considered shallow and sentimental, as ignoring its roots in human nature itself. These misapprehensions have, I believe, two sources. The first is a want of understanding of the requirements of allegory, and especially the need for impersonating separately in the fable qualities all of which may in reality be united in the same person. The second is the critics' forgetting the fact that for Shelley the gods are not real persons but mythological personifications, and in any case creations of the human mind. It is true that they represent real forces, for what man's mind creates plays an important part in his life. In "Prometheus Unbound" the gods are in large part evil; for they represent an established order that is reactionary, a principle of authority against which it is necessary to put up resistance. Jupiter is a name in this allegory for the force that actually reigns during the confinement of Prometheus and the exile of Asia. But he is in no sense to be identified with the supreme power of the universe, nor even with the Creator.

The confusion felt by Asia in her conference with Demogorgon serves to represent the usual confusion of mortals on these difficult questions of theology. When she asks who made the world, Demogorgon answers, God; and he makes the same answer when she inquires as to the creator of man's mind and affections. But when she asks who is responsible for pain and evil, he replies evasively, "He reigns."

She insists on knowing who it is that reigns; and then he relates the story of Saturn and of the investment of Jupiter with power by Prometheus and the subsequent torture of Prometheus for procuring benefits to man by his inventive power. At length, when Asia reminds the oracle how Jupiter had trembled at the curse of Prometheus, and wants to know if Jupiter too is a slave and who is his master, he replies:

> All spirits are enslaved which serve things evil:
> Thou knowest if Jupiter be such or no.

By this time Asia's confusion is at its height. If Jupiter is a slave to evil and no true god, then whom did Demogorgon refer to when he spoke of the creator of the world and men? "Whom calledst thou God?" she demands. And Demogorgon replies:

> I spoke but as ye speak.
> For Jove is the supreme of living things.

So Jove is not by any means to be identified with the Christian God or with the Creator. Men call him God, and they call the Creator God; and Demogorgon, in trying to answer the theological questions of Asia, speaks but as men speak. This is, I should say, a reflection of Shelley's agnosticism on the subject of God considered as the Creator. The origin of the world, he seems to say, is something beyond him. But with regard to its present government and eventual destiny, he has clearer knowledge. Asia wants to know who, if Jupiter is a slave to evil, is the power superior to him. "Who is the master of the slave?" The answer, as Demogorgon suggests, is difficult, hard to put in terms of human intelligence; but there is an answer.

> If the abysm
> Could vomit forth its secrets — but a voice
> Is wanting, the deep truth is imageless;

> For what would it avail to bid thee gaze
> On the revolving world? What to bid speak
> Fate, Time, Occasion, Chance, and Change? To these
> All things are subject but eternal Love.

Now, Asia is herself an impersonation of eternal Love, and in making this response to her question, Demogorgon is simply bidding her trust to the inspirations of her own heart. It is one of the most beautiful of dramatic devices thus to make of the hope of the world a humble inquirer after truth, to confront her in the allegory with the spirit of Destiny, and have her receive from his lips a confirmation of what she believes in her heart. Demogorgon lets her know that the sole power not subject to Fate, Time, Occasion, Chance, and Change is her own power of Love. And she replies:

> So much I asked before, and my heart gave
> The response thou hast given; and of such truths
> Each to himself must be the oracle.

As for Jupiter, then, while he may be for the moment the supreme of living things, he is not the Creator or the ultimate power of the universe. He is the spirit of tyrannical power, opposed to the freedom and progress of men, but still (as I suggest) representing one aspect of human nature. He was, we must remember, given his seat of power by Prometheus. Like all forces of good and evil, he was the creature of man's heart and will. When the change comes, man is freed from guilt and pain,

> Which were, for his will made or suffered them.

Briefly then, my interpretation of Shelley's intention in the poem is as follows. Human nature is represented by three figures, Jupiter, Prometheus, and Asia. Prometheus represents the inventive and progressive powers of man; to him are due all the "alleviations" of man's state; Jupiter, as

I have said, stands for the backward drag of selfish personal interest, tradition, and established authority. The two forces have come to a deadlock; and the power that can break it is Asia, type of love. But

> Asia waits in that far Indian vale.

Prometheus and Asia have been separated by the command of Jupiter; and the progressive energies of mankind cannot be realized till they are united again with the guiding ideal of love.

So long as this divorce continues, Jove reigns supreme of living things. But in the rule of Jupiter there is already a principle of decadence. This spirit of selfish evil is blind; he knows not the secret of the future, which is known to the prophetic Prometheus; and all his threats and tortures fail to force this secret from the Titan. In his determination to make his rule perpetual he blunders stupidly forward and marries Thetis, sometimes interpreted as the spirit of arrogance and pride. And so, in hopes of begetting an heir to his power, he actually provokes the fate that dethrones him. With dramatic irony he exults in the event that spells his ruin.

> Two mighty spirits, mingling, made a third
> Mightier than either, which, unbodied now,
> Between us floats, felt, although unbeheld,
> Waiting the incarnation, which ascends.

But when his heir appears, it is in the form of Demogorgon, who is Jove's nemesis, and ushers him down to his grave. Shelley is not here designating a single historical event, but an eternal process in the struggle between good and evil. The exigencies of the dramatic allegory require that it should be shown as taking place at a certain hour; but this is conceived of as one of those hours which are never over. And so Prometheus in his curse summons the hour—

> when thou must appear to be
> That which thou art internally;
> And after many a false and fruitless crime
> Scorn track thy lagging fall through boundless
>   space and time.

The same eternal hour brings the release of Prometheus, the return of Asia from exile, and the transformation of the world and man upon the sounding of her prophetic shell.

Thus we have what we might call the dialectic of the poem, the opposition of irreconcilable forces and the resolution of this conflict in terms of some force that transcends them. We might say that Jupiter represents the actual state of man in so far as it is evil, and Prometheus his potential state in so far as it is good, while Asia represents an ideal in terms of which the conflict is resolved. Man's life consists almost altogether in such conflict or tension of forces. Life is in a perpetual state of unbalance or instability, and we should hardly be conscious of our living at all if it were not for the struggle we carry on against reality, which fails to satisfy us, in favor of an ideal state, which challenges us to effort.

It is inevitable that poetry should, among its other functions, include as one of the most important the sensitive recording of this eternal dialectic. Indeed, the opinion might be hazarded that where poetry is most alive we are likely to find most active this play of conflicting attitudes, ideas, or impulses. The very contention of forces, resolved or unresolved, tends to give an effect of tension and vibrancy which is not found where the mind is absolutely at rest in a single point of view. We know that in the trilogy of Aeschylus, while the terms of the opposition are differently conceived from what they are in Shelley, and while the final resolution is altogether different, there is still a genuine opposition between two forces each of which is good in its way — the spirit of humane invention and the principle of authority. Still more, perhaps, in the tragedies of Sophocles the force of the drama lies, so far as our ethical sentiments are concerned, in the opposition of values the adjustment of whose claims is a matter of the utmost nicety.

The oppositions may be found in the realm of metaphysics, as so often in the poetry of Wordsworth and Shelley. In "Prometheus Unbound" it will be observed, contrary to much critical opinion, that Shelley insists on the paramountcy of the will. I have already quoted the passage in which Shelley declares that guilt and pain have been man's lot because his "will made or suffered them." Prometheus says to Jupiter:

> O'er all things but thyself I gave thee power,
> And my own will.

The worst that can befall man is for his will to be possessed by evil so that he becomes its victim.

> Evil, the immedicable plague, which, while
> Man looks on his creation like a God
> And sees that it is glorious, drives him on,
> The wreck of his own will, the scorn of earth. . . .

In man's transfigured state, his will, which can be a bad guide, is controlled to good ends by the power of love.

> His will, with all mean passions, bad delights,
> And selfish cares, its trembling satellites,
> A spirit ill to guide, but mighty to obey,
> Is as a tempest-wingèd ship, whose helm
> Love rules, through waves which dare not overwhelm,
> Forcing life's wildest shores to own its sovereign sway.

Now, it is well known that Shelley was at an earlier period a somewhat fanatical proponent of necessitarianism. And even in "Prometheus" there are passages suggesting that he is still clinging to the doctrine of necessity. Asia and Panthea are fatally drawn to the cave of Demogorgon, and on the way pass through a deep, voluptuous wood, where the very echoes exert a compulsion on them.

> There those enchanted eddies play
>   Of echoes, music-tongued, which draw,
>   By Demogorgon's mighty law,
>   With melting rapture, or sweet awe,
> All spirits on that secret way;
>   As inland boats are driven to Ocean
> Down streams made strong with mountain thaw:
> And first there comes a gentle sound
> To those in talk or slumber bound,
>   And wakes the destined soft emotion, —
> Attracts, impels them; those who saw
>   Say from the breathing earth behind
>   There steams a plume-uplifting wind
> Which drives them on their path, while they
>   Believe their own swift wings and feet
> The sweet desires within obey:
> And so they float upon their way,
> Until, still sweet, but loud and strong,
> The storm of wind is driven along,
>   Sucked up and hurrying: as they fleet
>   Behind, its gathering billows meet
> And to the fatal mountain bear
> Like clouds amid the yielding air.

The fatal mountain is the place where Demogorgon has his cave — Demogorgon, symbol of destiny or fate. All spirits are attracted and impelled toward that destination by certain enchanted echoes which awake "the destined soft emotion"; and while they think they are obeying "the sweet desires within," they are actually following a determined course.

It is easy to say that Shelley is stating here an opinion directly contradictory to others in which he asserts the importance of the will in guiding human action. It is much more reasonable to say that Shelley in apparently conflict-ing passages shows two sides of a coin which, however often and ingeniously you toss it, will continue to have two sides. "Will" is one of the most indispensable and most ambiguous of words. We all experience daily and faithfully acknowl-edge the existence of voluntary action, the process of mak-ing up our minds and choosing among alternatives. But when we inquire coolly as to what actually goes on when we make up our minds, how the choice of alternatives is affected by the character we possess, and how the character we possess is affected by those universal trends which we call the laws of nature, we begin to grow less dogmatic in our assertions. If any of the philosophers or theologians had worked out this problem in a completely satisfactory way, and without begging some of the questions at issue, we should be more ready to condemn the poet for his indeci-siveness. But the nature of the will is one of those subjects on which the more you reflect the less you are inclined to flat-footed assertion.

If Shelley had anywhere asserted the *freedom* of the will, we might complain of his references to fatal echoes impel-ling us upon our destined course. But the one thing a cau-tious thinker is least inclined to assert is the freedom of the will. The primacy of the will, yes, the responsibility of the will, yes, the need of right guidance for the will, yes — but the freedom of the will, no — not if you mean by that, that the will exists in a vacuum, out of relation to the rest of our nature and the world. One hesitates to assert the free-dom of the will in that sense, because it seems to imply that the acts of the will are arbitrary and without reasonable or intelligible motivation. That of course was not the posi-tion of Shelley, who had made such a resolute effort to reconcile his platonic idealism with his faith in the natural order as envisaged by contemporary science, and, like

Wordsworth, to combine into one system of thought the associationism of the eighteenth century with the intuitionalism of the seventeenth.

The dogmatizing moralist can offer a much neater solution of these problems because, in his singleness of mind, he can overlook so many truths that are obvious to the philosopher or the man of the world. The poet can often be convicted of inconsistency because he is so fond of turning the object round and round in many lights, bringing to view facets of the truth hard to reconcile by any logic or any psychology at our command. But that is a main source of his appeal to those who take the truths of experience as they come, leaving it to later reflection to make them conformable to logic or invent a psychology whose refinements will be equal to comprehending them in one system. The reader of poetry has a poetic mind, which balks not at mysteries where they are approved by his own experience; which finds, indeed, that they give to a poem that dynamism he has felt in life itself.

It is for this reason that readers of any maturity are delighted with the performance of Byron in "Don Juan." They enjoy the perpetual counterpoint of romanticism and cynicism, of high and low, which is suggested by the word "burlesque." They appreciate the endless resourcefulness and versatility with which he develops the dramatic oppositions inherent in his theme as he conceives it. They relish the sweep of his mind, and they range with him in happy vagabondage over whole kingdoms of thought and feeling. They are grateful to him for his candor and his wit. And they leave for another day the ultimate ethical questions which he may have ignored, knowing that, if he cannot satisfy the deepest aspirations of the soul, they are always at liberty to turn to someone who can, be it Shelley or Emerson, Milton or Goethe, Dante or Saint John.

And now let me give you another instance of emotional dialectic from romantic poetry — from a somewhat lower range of romantic feeling than that represented by "Prometheus." Keats's "Lamia" is a poem that has been a stumbling-block to a number of critics. And that largely because, in their anxious moralism, they have been troubled by the prominence in Keats of the sensuous or fleshly element and have felt impelled to show a progress in him away from sensuous hedonism toward an ethical philosophy predicated on the subordination of the senses. Some of them have been very ingenious in tracing this progress and can tell you just what ratio the "sensual" bears to the "philosophic" in January 1817 or July 1818 or October 1819. Some of them will have it that "Lamia," written in the summer of 1819, indicates the triumph in his thinking of reason or morality over the sensual enticements of fleshly love. But perhaps a greater number of critics sadly note, on the contrary, that the poem shows a relapse from rationality into the lower level of uncritical emotion. And both schools agree that the poem is to be taken as a serious ethical pronouncement.

Keats, surrounded as he was by professional proponents of social benevolence like Leigh Hunt, and impressed as he was by the philosophical profundity of his admired Wordsworth, did feel the urge to give to his poetry a more philosophical and idealistic character than it naturally had. But Keats knew very well both that he did not have a native bent for philosophical speculation and that he was a promising poet in spite of that.

> What though I am not wealthy in the dower
> Of spanning wisdom; though I do not know
> The shiftings of the mighty winds that blow
> Hither and thither all the changing thoughts
> Of man: though no great minist'ring reason sorts
> Out the dark mysteries of human souls
> To clear conceiving: yet there ever rolls

A vast idea before me, and I glean
Therefrom my liberty; thence too I've seen
The end and aim of Poesy.

These lines occur in "Sleep and Poetry," a piece written in 1816, at a time when he was already much occupied with the story of Diana and her earthly lover. It was in the following year, in "Endymion," that he presumably made his most determined effort to fix the "vast idea" that rolled before him. The product was a tangle of charming imagery and fantastic fable, in which the idea is stretched so thin that some good critics decline to admit that there is properly speaking any idea there. The one thought that is clearest in the poem is that sacred and profane love are not irreconcilable, but rather identical, as shown in the discovery that the Indian maid is one and the same with Diana.

Well, Keats did not have the sort of mind that is suited to this kind of undertaking. But he had a very good, a clear and objective mind; and in particular he had a fine understanding of many points in normal psychology that are admirably suited to poetic treatment. He understood the dialectic of emotion and the difficulty which feeling has in justifying itself before the bar of cold reason. That is his subject in "Lamia." But the subject is not as simple as it is sometimes thought to be. And while, in "Lamia," the representative of feeling suffers defeat at the hands of "cold philosophy" and the youth who is the battleground of their conflict becomes its victim, it is far from right to say that Keats is therefore giving his approval to cold philosophy or signifying his allegiance to reason as against emotion; still less that he is showing in this poem the evil character of sensual passion. But on the other hand, it is only a little less wrong to say that the poem is a flat repudiation of reason as destructive of emotion. Even so we need not conclude, as some have done, that Keats did not know what he thought, or that, because there are contradictions inherent in his attitude toward this affair, the poem lacks unity of thought or feeling. The unity of thought is found in its contradictions; that is what I mean when I speak of its dialectic.

The subject is taken from Burton's *Anatomy of Melancholy;* and Burton, while he speaks of the heroine as a serpent or Lamia and refers her to the general category of evil spirits, has nothing to say of the vampire-like proclivities ordinarily associated with lamias. Still less is there any hint of this side of her nature in Keats's rendering. Lamia is, to be sure, a snake-woman, a creature of enchantment. In describing her appearance as a serpent, Keats offers three different hypotheses as to her actual nature, all doubtless taken from current folklore. She was —

> So rainbow-sided, touch'd with miseries,
> She seem'd, at once, some penanc'd lady elf,
> Some demon's mistress, or the demon's self.

If she were either a penanc'd lady elf or some demon's mistress, she might well be more the victim of evil magic than herself an evil being. There are plenty of snake-women who are snakes only in seeming and as the result of a spell that can be removed by the love of a man. As for Lamia's actual conduct, there is nothing malicious about it, nothing wrong except for her suppression of the truth, and nothing peculiar except her way of raising up palaces and feasts by magic. Her deception is not undertaken with any evil designs on Lycius but simply because she has fallen into a swooning love for him. It was a great delight to her to be released from the sore penance of a serpent form, and so released she was not merely a maid "more beautiful than ever twisted braid," but one deeply learned in the lore of love,

As though in Cupid's college she had spent
Sweet days a lovely graduate.

The principal change made by Keats in Burton's story is
his addition of the Hermes episode, which is conceived in a
tone of clear pagan amorousness calculated to invest the
affair of Lamia and Lycius with its own sympathetic enthusiasm. Hermes is shown rosy and godlike in pursuit of
a nymph, who has so enthralled his fancy that when he
thinks of her,

a celestial heat
Burnt from his winged heels to either ear,
That from a whiteness, as the lily clear,
Blush'd into roses 'mid his golden hair,
Fallen in jealous curls about his shoulders bare.

Unfortunately his nymph, who is possessed of magic powers, has taken to making herself invisible in order to escape
the unwelcome attentions of Satyrs, Fauns, and blear'd
Silenuses. Such is the situation when the infatuated god en-
counters the infatuated Lamia and they exchange favors.
He agrees to release her from the serpent form on condition that she restore his nymph to visibility. No sooner said
than done, and he actually beholds his nymph in the flesh.

It was no dream; or say a dream it was,
Real are the dreams of Gods, and smoothly pass
Their pleasures in a long immortal dream.

Now that, I take it, is as serious a statement of Keats's
feeling as there is to be found in the poem. Not solemn-
serious, for that is something Keats is not likely to be in
his dealing with Greek mythology. This was for him a
world of playful fancy, where the desires of the heart may
sport unchecked by the anxious moralities of daily life in
Georgian England. "Endymion" is one long excursion into
this adolescent world of wish-fulfillment, and whenever in

that poem he tries to sound a more strenuous or Platonic note he signally fails to bring conviction. His most convincing god is one of his own creation, the Psyche of his ode, patroness of roving fancy and of love. In his reference to the loves of Hermes, the light and fanciful touch is not absent, nor even a trace of wistful humor. But the dominant note is that of admiration and envy. There are in Keats enough passages of warm praise for love, even when

> 'tis understood
> The mere commingling of passionate breath

to keep us from doubting the deep sincerity of his feeling about the Hermes affair.

> It was no dream; or say a dream it was,
> Real are the dreams of Gods.

Just here the dialectic of the poem makes its appearance. Our emotions are likely ever to involve an element of illusion. They too often pass like dreams and leave us, as Keats's knight-at-arms was left, "on the cold hillside." That is the sad feature of our mortal estate. With gods it is different. Such is the very meaning of pagan godhead. Their dreams are real where ours are illusory. And it is not that dreams are evil, that emotion is bad, that love is something to be disparaged; but that with men emotion has no standing in the world of rationality.

> Do not all charms fly
> At the mere touch of cold philosophy?

The lines that follow give a clue to the sentimental lengths to which his disparagement of reason would carry Keats when he was in the mood. Keats is even willing, in pursuit of this theme, to blame Newton for reducing the rainbow to its prismatic colors and so dispersing its poetry.

> There was an awful rainbow once in heaven:
> We know her woof, her texture; she is given

> In the dull catalogue of common things.
> Philosophy would clip an Angel's wings,
> Conquer all mysteries by rule and line,
> Empty the haunted air, and gnomed mine —
> Unweave a rainbow, as it erstwhile made
> The tender-person'd Lamia melt into a shade.

It is not necessary to conclude that John Keats was an enemy of reason and science. It was because he was so much under their spell that he could resent them when, as in this fabled instance, they came into conflict with emotion. He was not an enemy to reason, but he was a friend to love. He was a poet, and in this poem, in keeping with that character, his sympathies are all on the side of the charms of love, which are represented by Lamia. Consider how disparaging are his references to the philosopher. He is several times referred to as a sophist, and Lycius reproaches him in the end with all his "impious proud-heart sophistries, unlawful magic, and enticing lies." That is one view of reason. But in his own view Apollonius is an honest sage. He has no choice but to expose the cheat. And to Lycius's reproaches he answers, with sturdy dignity:

> from every ill
> Of life I have preserv'd thee to this day,
> And shall I see thee made a serpent's prey?

The opposition is sharply drawn. There can be no truce between the illusion of the heart and the cold reckoning of the head. The serpent-woman vanishes and the lover's heart stops beating.

There is one aspect of the case which is heavily underlined by Keats. It is, again, an original turn given by him to the story, and we cannot afford to ignore it in our interpretation of his thought. The second part begins with the famous characterization of love:

Love in a hut, with water and a crust,
Is — Love, forgive us! — cinders, ashes, dust;
Love in a palace is perhaps at last
More grievous torment than a hermit's fast: —
That is a doubtful tale from faery land,
Hard for the non-elect to understand.
Had Lycius liv'd to hand his story down,
He might have given the moral a fresh frown,
Or clench'd it quite: but too short was their bliss
To breed distrust and hate, that make the soft voice hiss.

Love is a difficult state to maintain; under whatever circumstances, it contains the seeds of its own destruction. This is not the only passage in the poem in which Keats dwells on the elements of pain which are in the very nature of things involved in this experience. The maiden with whom Lycius falls in love is, we are told,

in the lore
Of love deep learned to the red heart's core:
Not one hour old, yet of sciential brain
To unperplex bliss from its neighbour pain;
Define their pettish limits, and estrange
Their points of contact, and swift counterchange;
Intrigue with the specious chaos, and dispart
Its most ambiguous atoms with sure art.

It is no man unacquainted with the psychology of love who thus describes its devious and tantalizing ways, its subtleties and sophistries. And in his management of the conclusion Keats has given one striking instance of the ways in which the most fortunate love may prove its own undoing.

For anything he shows, Lycius's dream of amorous bliss might have lasted forever if he had not been seized with the perverse desire to publish to the world his happiness and pride. It was his vanity that provoked disaster. In the very midst of his enjoyment he begins to think of how he can

cash in on it in a worldly way. Lamia at once perceives that
something is wrong —

> Because he mus'd beyond her, knowing well
> That but a moment's thought is passion's passing bell.

She accuses him of having deserted her in his heart and insists on knowing the subject of his thought. And he replies.

> My thoughts! shall I unveil them? Listen then!
> What mortal hath a prize, that other men
> May be confounded and abash'd withal,
> But lets it sometimes pace abroad majestical,
> And triumph, as in thee I should rejoice
> Amid the hoarse alarm of Corinth's voice.
> Let my foes choke, and my friends shout afar,
> While through the thronged streets your bridal car
> Wheels round its dazzling spokes.

Thus it is the vulgar wish to show off his good fortune that
leads Lycius to this fatal step. It is not his love the poet con-
demns, but the gross element of worldliness that enters
into it.

> O senseless Lycius! Madman! wherefore flout
> The silent-blessing fate, warm cloister'd hours
> And show to common eyes these secret bowers?

This is not the only reef on which love may founder.
Keats's thought is wider than that. It is but one dramatic
illustration of his central theme —

> That but a moment's thought is passion's passing bell.

That is a theme which might be treated in several different
ways. It might be treated in the neoclassic manner, in satire
or moral essay. Keats follows the romantic vein. This is no
thought in which the mind rejoices, except as the mind always takes satisfaction in its own discoveries, however dis-
illusioning. The poem is written frankly from the point of
view of sentiment, but the poet is so vividly conscious of

the opposing point of view, the contradiction is so sharp and uncompromising, that the strings of his spirit are taut with the strain and his verses ring with the poignant dialectic.

For his statement and counterstatement he has no reconciling synthesis to offer. And this is in general characteristic of Keats. Where he has undertaken such a synthesis, as in "Hyperion," he has seldom been successful. "Hyperion" was dropped almost before he had got it seriously under way. And he dropped it, I imagine, not so much because he was dissatisfied with his version of the Miltonic style as because he realized that his subject could not be made to carry the weight of philosophic intention which he had hoped. In this failure to provide a resolution for his dialectic oppositions, Keats is in a class with Byron, however much they may differ in other ways, and in contrast to Shelley and Wordsworth. This difference you may express in various terms, according to your disposition. You may say that Keats and Byron are more realistic than Wordsworth and Shelley, or more hardheaded; you may even say they are more clearheaded, more "sound." I should prefer to say simply that Keats and Byron were temperamentally less fitted to leaven the reality they encountered with the ideal which they visioned.

But more than that, I am convinced that Wordsworth and Shelley both had speculative endowments of a high order, whereas Byron and Keats are vastly better poets than they are philosophers. Most fascinating are the regions in which poetry and philosophy meet on equal and harmonious terms. The nature poetry of Wordsworth is particularly rich in illustrations of the play of dialectic. For Wordsworth managed to ride together more of the wild horses of the mind than any poet of his day. His effort was to drive in teams science and religion, the natural and the spiritual, mind and heart, objective and subjective, plain understanding and intuitive vision. Matthew Arnold was inclined to disparage the philosophical side of Wordsworth's work; but he was thinking of "The Excursion" with its pietistic moralisms, its tangled effort to justify the ways of God to man. Here we must agree with Arnold, but we cannot agree with him in ignoring that side of Wordsworth's thought, where he was less confused by conventional loyalties — his philosophy of nature as set forth in "Tintern Abbey" and "The Prelude" and implied in numerous poems of his early maturity. Wordsworth's views were given in the terms of his day and in the terms of poetry. They have not the abstract precision or logical coherence of Hume's or Kant's. And they could not be reproduced today without a considerable adaptation to the terms of contemporary thought. But they represent aspects of the truth and of our human reaction to the truth which are bound to have significance and imaginative appeal so long as we are men.

And even yet as you read Wordsworth the page is alive with concepts each one of which is daringly and precariously compounded of mental positions in some sense antithetical. These oppositions are not of his invention, and they are not simply the evidence of mental confusion or inconsistency. They are aspects of the truth which must be recognized by any enlightened and penetrating mind that has faced experience with seriousness and candor. It may be necessary at times, in the interest of practical simplification, to let one aspect go and cleave to another; and this may be done out of mere weariness of mind. But whenever freshness returns to the mind and it feels free to contemplate the truth in all its multifariousness, one finds that the opposed positions are still there, as insistently distinct as green and red, and yet somehow united in actual experience. This is one of the most challenging features of our mental life, and the poet who can do justice not merely to the oppositions inherent in our thinking but also to the compelling need we have for wholeness and integrity has done us a double service. He has given us the truth of experience in its living fullness and diversity, and at the same time he has bound together the disunited tendrils of our being. He has restored us, in Wordsworth's own feeling words,

To those sweet counsels between head and heart

without which we should be lost in an alien world.

And so it seems we have come a long way beyond those simple satisfactions which it is an added joy to realize in rhythmed words. We have seen how great a yield our very pain of heart may bring when we can give it outward and esthetic form, relieving so the pent-up and burdened spirit, and from our personal grief shaping an object for impersonal contemplation and delight. And finally we have seen how the very divisions and contradictions of the mind have their contribution to make to the satisfaction taken in poetic art, reflecting as they do that heightened consciousness, that sense of tension and excitement, which is the most defining feature of life itself — of life at any level, but especially of life on its highest and most rewarding levels.